A TRAVELLER
IN CHINA

A TRAVELLER
IN CHINA
Christina Dodwell

BEAUFORT BOOKS
Publishers • New York

Author's note

I should like to thank Dodwell International, of the Inchcape Group, for giving some financial support to my journey, and I should also like to thank the people of China for their kindness along the way.   CD

Library of Congress Cataloging-in-Publication Data

Dodwell, Christina, 1951-
A traveller in China.

1. China—Description and travel—1976-
2. Dodwell, Christina, 1951-   —Journeys—China.
I. Title.
DS712.D63   1986   915.1′045   85-28781
ISBN 0-8253-0371-0

Published in the United States by Beaufort Books Publishers, New York.

Printed in the U.S.A.   First American Edition

10   9   8   7   6   5   4   3   2

Contents

1   A bus stop in Tartary   9
2   Along the Silk Road   13
3   The crossroads of Asia   22
4   A canoe on Lake Karakol   28
5   Desert cities   41
6   Heaven Lake and solitude   50
7   Into the Black Gobi   59
8   Graves and warriors   70
9   Bicycle philosophy   76
10 Along the Yellow River   82
11 Grandmother's footsteps   88
12 Into Tibet   99
13 The biggest lake in China   107
14 Taer'si pilgrimage   111
15 Tea shops in Chengdu   118
16 The stone forest at Shilin   122
17 The Burma Road to Dali   129
18 The Sacred Mountain   133
19 Yangtse rapids   140
20 Invitation to the waltz   147
21 The Dragon Boat Race   152
22 Paddling into a watercolour   155

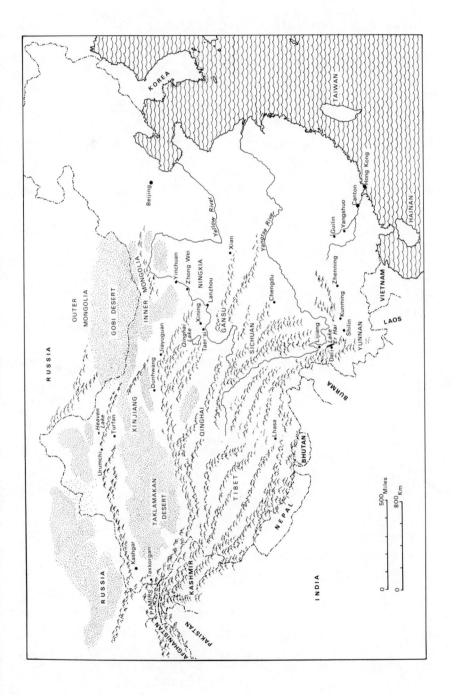

1   A bus stop in Tartary

I flew into Tartary because it was where I wanted to catch a bus. Xinjiang Autonomous Region, as this north-western edge of China is known today, is isolated by the highest mountains and the largest desert in the world, linked to the outside by the thread of one of history's oldest trade routes, the Silk Road, travelled by Marco Polo. All the same, I had no great romantic expectations of Urumchi, its state capital. Peter Fleming mentions two banquets in 1916 and 1928 where the guests were beheaded one by one, which may account for the verdict of the missionary travellers Mildred Cable and Francesca French, who were there in the 1930s and wrote categorically: 'No one enjoys life in Urumchi; no one leaves the town with regret, and it is full of people who are only there because they cannot get permission to leave.'

Nowadays it is still an ugly city. Its sprawling industrial areas produce so much smoky pollution that one can seldom see the snowy mountains which fringe this part of the Gobi Desert. My first task on arriving in Urumchi was to find a permitted way of getting to Kashgar. Foreigners entering China need an alien's travel card which allows them to visit only the areas specified on it, but these can be officially added to at any time. One's movements are controlled by the Public Security Office who keep a list of places which are 'open' to foreigners. Usually these are cities, but some interesting rural areas have opened recently, and it was these parts I hoped to find. One newly opened city was Kashgar, fabled crossroads of Asia. I could have flown direct, but I wanted to travel the Silk Road myself and experience the desert, which was why I was finding my way to Urumchi's public bus depot that day at the beginning of May.

There is a daily bus service to Kashgar, and it takes four days. The clerk didn't want to sell me a ticket because, as she said, it's an arduous journey and the night halts are at truck-drivers' inns. But she finally agreed and after warning me that the back afforded a very bumpy ride, sold me a front window seat.

Before leaving England I had spent a couple of months acquiring some basic Mandarin; speaking Chinese, although very haltingly, proved invaluable on this occasion, but in general I was amazed to find how few people who live here can speak Chinese. Whenever I asked for directions people made me wait until they could find someone who understood Chinese. And looking around I could see that the faces were not of Han (Chinese) descent. The men's beards were thicker than Chinese beards grow, and their hair was not quite so black. Their faces were aquiline, some weatherbeaten by desert life, and some with whiter skin than mine, with features that varied widely. Being Central Asians they belong to various nomadic races, such as Uighur, Mongol, Kazakh and Khirgiz, and there are also settled emigrés, including White Russians.

When we say Chinese, we usually think of all those who live in China as one race, the race being the Han majority from eastern and northern Chinese stock, their name taken from the powerful dynasty that ruled China for four centuries from 200 BC. But from a Chinese perspective one has to take into account the fifty-four other ethnic groups who are culturally different from the Han, but whose land has been annexed by China. They may comprise less than a tenth of China's total population, yet they occupy about sixty per cent of the territory. Some are nomadic, some are hill tribes. All have distinctive ways of life and I was particularly eager to visit as many of these groups as possible on the remote fringes of China's north-west and south-west border, with their colourful customs and costumes.

As I searched for a hotel permitted to accept foreigners, someone wrote the directions on a piece of paper. To my surprise the writing was not in ideographic Chinese characters, it was in Arabic calligraphy, and everyone could read and understand it, except me. Then I realised that the shop signs are also written in Arabic, and the bus stop signs. A girl put me on to a town bus and told the driver where to put me off. Standing room only, swelteringly hot, packed tightly, it was a double-length articulated bus, a heavy load for its engine which, between stops, gasped and shuddered to a halt. In response, the driver picked up the can of water that I'd assumed to be for refilling the radiator, and poured it over the engine block. Within minutes the engine had re-started.

The hotel offered rooms or dormitories; I opted for a four-bed dormitory which I shared with three Hong Kong tourists. They spoke Cantonese, not Mandarin, and very little English. For supper I went to a noodle stall in the night market. The chef stood bashing the noodles out by hand, looping the strands around his fingers and thrashing them against a flour-coated table while pulling his hands further apart. The noodle ropes stretched evenly without breaking, and stretched again every time he re-looped them, until they had reached the required thinness. My supper was noodle soup with chopped greens, mutton and hot chili. A friendly crowd of Uighur and Huizi gathered to watch me eat. One Hui man told me that he could speak five languages: Hui, Uighur, Kazakh, Mongolian and Chinese. He also said he owned two horses and a sheep. Another man swapped a hard-boiled egg with me for some tobacco. Several of the market stalls were selling dried fruit so I bought a quantity of dried peaches, apricots, and raisins. The raisins were the sweetest I've ever tasted, almost crystalline. There wasn't much else for sale – few vegetables, though the radishes were the size of large carrots.

Under Mao's regime, market trading was banned as being a capitalist idea. The communist economy could not admit to being lacking; shortage reflected poorly on the Party. But producing for the good of the state is not half as appealing an incentive as producing for yourself and family. Party ideology lost the battle with human nature, and since the end of the Cultural Revolution people have gradually been allowed to cultivate private plots, in addition to their collective work. Private ownership of plots and livestock has in turn led to the re-emergence of the open market, doing a thriving business.

At 8 p.m. the sun was setting; it doesn't get dark until about ten, since the Beijing clock is standard across 3,000 miles. There are no time zones in China. A group of people were watching the antics of a monkey show. The monkey stood nearly three feet tall, dressed in a ragged skirt, and it walked, danced and somersaulted to the accompaniment of chants and a gong. The gong was so worn that it had a hole in the middle, and the cloth-topped baton made only a tinny rattling thud. The long-haired old man who wielded it chanted in a reedy, unmelodious voice, while the monkey went to a wooden chest and took out a hat and a white-faced mask with a gruesome expression like a Chinese door god. Continuing its antics, the monkey clowned and imitated people, and for a grand finale it somersaulted in the air cleanly feet over head, which the crowd applauded with enthusiasm.

A tin dish was handed around for donations and I put in a little money-note, which was seized by the next person and examined by a knot of people. They weren't looking at the amount (which was small), they were comparing it to their notes, which are different. Now I understood what travellers meant by 'funny money'; mine was the funny stuff, being Foreign Exchange Certificated (FEC), not the same as the Chinese people's own notes (reminbi).

One man pocketed my money and put in the equivalent value of reminbi, but the monkey-owner got upset and demanded my money from him. From the ensuing argument I gathered that my FEC were at a premium because they can be used to buy articles which are not available to ordinary Chinese. The argument blazed on, so I halted it by donating a second note.

Before going to sleep that night I wrote up my diary and consulted my map to see how Xinjiang and the Gobi fitted in. Xinjiang Autonomous Region occupies one sixth of China and shares frontiers with Russia, Mongolia, Afghanistan, Pakistan, Kashmir and Tibet. Xinjiang may sound large but it's much smaller than the Gobi Desert which covers and extends far beyond it. The Gobi is nearly 2,000 miles long and up to 1,200 miles wide. The desert between here and Kashgar is a vast basin called Taklamakan (which means 'Go in and you won't come out'). It has a bad reputation as one of the worst and most dangerous deserts in the world, with appallingly violent sand-storms. Entire camel caravans have been known to vanish there without trace. Our bus route would follow the northern edge of the Taklamakan Basin, along beside the Tien Shan mountain range.

This is the route of the Silk Road which linked China to Rome, one of the oldest of the world's great thoroughfares. But it's misleading to think of it as one single road since it had arms that split and re-joined, giving alternative routes around arid desert and temporary war zones, and branches that led north to Russia and south to the Indian coast. Its name sprang from the Romans' passion for silk. The canny Chinese kept the secret of its production to themselves for centuries. The Romans thought that silk grew on trees.

2 Along the Silk Road

On arrival at 7 a.m. at the bus depot I was greeted by a scene of commotion. Scores of people with bundles, boxes and suitcases were trying to haul their luggage on to the bus roofrack, with much noise and clamour of voices. We weren't allowed to get on the bus until 7.30 and from the jostling crowd it didn't appear likely that we had each got a reserved seat. One sure thing was that the bus would be full.

At the front of the crowd was a Turki peasant woman with an injured knee, she was whimpering with pain, and when we boarded the bus she took the front seat next to mine. On being told by the conductor that her seat was at the back (the bumpiest ride) she began wailing her agony. I was surprised because peasant women usually show a more stoic acceptance of pain, but I noticed that her agony disappeared quickly after the conductor had moved on.

I was the only European; several of the passengers were moon-faced Hans, wearing drab green or blue Mao clothes. The rest were Turki or Uighur. The men wore skull-caps embroidered with silk or gold thread. Some of the women wore head-shawls with skull-caps on top. Each main oasis in this area has its own distinctive embroidered hat pattern and you can tell a person's home town by his skull-cap.

A violent argument broke out between two men, one seemed to be trying to force the other to get off the bus. They shouted angrily in fast tongue-clicking speech, and people from all over the bus joined in yelling insults, while the conductor called for silence. The argument got more heated. I was intrigued by the force of anger being displayed. In our society it would have turned into a brawl long ago, but these two were maximising the art of verbal abuse. The quarrel raged for an hour, the bus-driver refused to start, while the sun rose higher and the air grew dusty. Finally the men did grab hold of each other and start to fight. One of them was thrown off the bus, and we set out along the road towards Kashgar. I felt pleased to leave Urumchi. As we drew away from the belching factory chimneys we emerged on to a flat plain, sandy but with scrub plants, and far beyond the flatness on both horizons were snow-capped mountains. It seemed strange to be in a hot desert with such a view.

The man who'd been fighting now began to sing a mournful-sounding dirge, which droned on for half an hour before he suddenly became merry and broke into more tuneful song. The sandy wastes gave way to arid grasslands, where we saw a herd of camels. They were in poor condition after the winter and their humps were flopped emptily over sideways. When they have been grazing for a few weeks their humps may start to grow fat and sit upright. Two of the females had fluffy baby camels; they stood gawking and terrified by the sight of our bus which trundled slowly along with its roof-tarpaulin flapping in the wind. The road went into a gorge and out on to another plain, bare of vegetation, where windswept cliffs were scored into deep gulleys. The cliffs seemed near then far, changing colour as the sun moved to its zenith.

We stopped for lunch in a dusty oasis town where numerous cafés vying for business provided us with a choice of dishes. I chose *pilau*, the national dish of the Uighurs, a delicious though greasy fry-up of chopped lamb, rice, carrots, onions, sultanas, raisins and spices. The only problem was the amount of sand in it which kept crunching between my teeth. I wondered if this was a foretaste of what was to come.

In the afternoon the singing man continued his semi-tuneful chant, and the other passengers nodded off to sleep, though I found that impossible with the lurching and swaying of the bus. My neighbour's head kept falling on my shoulder which didn't bother me but she awoke and felt very embarrassed about it. So I folded my cardigan as a pillow between us, but she sat bolt upright and refused to make use of it. She couldn't speak any Chinese, only Uighur, and I realised that if I wanted to talk with my fellow passengers, I was going to have to learn a bit of Uighur.

As I understood the theory, the spoken Uighur language has amazingly complex verb tenses including future potentials and the hearsay-compound-present, which means 'one is under-stood to be/be doing . . .' Chinese is simple because the verb doesn't change. To speak in the past tense you just add '*le*' to the sentence, or put in a time reference. To make a question you just add '*ma?*', although *ma* can also mean mother or horse according to the tone used.

Though there were several Han on the bus, I hadn't spoken to them since the Uighur people had claimed me as their own property, and I discovered the Uighur do not like the Han. They still tend to see them as unwelcome overlords. There were massive riots in the early 1980s in west Xinjiang. Our bus would pass near those towns, but nowadays all seems quiet.

Outside the open window was a vastness of grey shale. Twisted skeletons of donkeys lay alongside the road. Some corpses still had skin and fur on, mummified by the dryness of the desert air. The road took us west into low mountains of craggy shale. Up for two hours then down into a basin where dust-devils whirled. The huts in an oasis we passed through were half-buried under drifts of sand. Over the next couple of hours the desert was undulating with small mountain ranges, some grey-black, and some red, green, yellow and cream-coloured. Gritty sand; even the sky was gritty.

Some of the dust-devils spun in pairs. I was craning around and changing sides of the bus to get a better look at them, and finally ascertained that in each pair the devils were spinning opposite ways. A Han fellow-passenger told me that they spin different ways because they are male and female. Kwei (devil spirits) are believed to inhabit the desert, visible only in their dusty capes.

The bus passengers began waking up from their afternoon naps, and to amuse my neighbour I showed her my postcards of England and photographs of my family. This is one of my ways of breaking the conversational ice where language is difficult. It worked in Africa and Papua New Guinea too. Many pairs of hands suddenly appeared from behind our seats, eagerly seizing pictures to take for everyone on the bus to see. One man asked if he could keep a picture of a red double-decker London bus, and since I'd brought spare copies of several cards, I gave it to him.

There was little to compare between the red London bus and the faded coach we travelled on. It stopped seldom and it moved very slowly. When it stopped for the passengers to go and relieve themselves, everyone got out and stood or squatted near the bus; they seemed to have no need for privacy. I was glad I was wearing a skirt, not jeans. The Turki women wear a knee-length tunic over baggy trousers. Being Moslems, their arms and heads are covered. They asked me why my head wasn't covered so I explained that I'm not Moslem. What surprised me was that I never saw them stop to say their prayers in the prescribed Moslem fashion.

In the evening we stopped at 8 p.m. at a truckers' hotel, and all the passengers went to a small barred window reception where they clamoured for beds; all waving one-yuan notes (33p) and trying to push these in through the window, behind which a clerk was issuing bed tickets. It was too crowded for me and I stood back to wait. Suddenly the office door opened and another clerk pulled me inside, shoved a ticket into my hand and pointed to a women's dormitory. I was grateful for the preferential treatment, and other people were helpful about where to find cold running water, and boiling water for the room's tea-thermos. The ladies' loo was a series of holes in a concrete platform, with outer walls and low partitions. The women stared at me with curiosity. The trough below the platform collects the waste which is later scooped into buckets and poured on the fields as fertiliser.

The dormitory had six hard wooden beds – a bit spartan but I was glad I'd brought my sleeping bag for extra padding. And the night was fairly cold. At about midnight some men came in with a flashlight and shook me until I woke up. They shone the light in my face and asked to see my travel permit, but after checking that it was in order, they went away.

We were up and aboard the bus by 7.30 the next morning. People who were late got jeered at by those waiting. The road led along below the foothills of the Tien-Shan range. Ice-capped mountains were never long out of sight above the barren desert hills. Streams coming from the melting snows ran a short way into the desert before spreading into marshes or salt flats and disappearing into the sand. Many streams and rivers enter the Taklamakan Basin but none flow out to the sea. It was the existence of such streams and ponds that made it possible for ancient travellers and camel caravans to pass along the Silk Road, on a route which was marked by a cairn every *li* (roughly two thirds of a mile). Two thousand years ago when the Silk Road became important with increased trade, some of the watering places developed into cities, centres of wealth and feudal kingdoms. Nowadays the stone cairns and rutted track have been replaced by a good road; partly dirt and partly asphalt, and it's used by a lot of traffic. Gone are the camel caravans; the traffic is trucks, but not Western trucks, these are made in Poland, Russia, East Germany and Japan.

In the old days, besides silk, the westbound cargo was weapons, ironware, lacquerwork, furs, ceramics, mirrors and jade; and coming east one would have seen gold, precious stones, ivory, textiles and glass. The modern consignments going west are coal, rubber tyres, oil drums, building materials, scrap iron and metal; while trucks coming east carry live donkeys, bales of goatskins, hides and wool, and bundles of straw and dry reeds, some so long that they trail behind the trucks and sweep the road.

The desert, now a salty alkaline plain of crusty white, has also changed, in the way that deserts are always changing with the wind and passing of centuries. In this Taklamakan desert the alterations caused by the mountain streams' drying up or changing course over the years have accounted for the rise and decline of many vanished cities. At one time the cities had been prosperous centres of trade, study and worship, richly nourished with fresh fruit and vegetables from their advanced irrigation systems. Prosperity produced lavish temples.

One such ancient site is at Kucha, where the bus driver stopped to re-fuel and do engine repairs, which gave us passengers the time to take a stroll locally. The temple frescoes discovered here are said to be the finest in Turkestan. They show scenes from Buddha's life, painted with the brilliant ultramarine coveted by Renaissance artists. None of the artwork is Chinese – the temples date from AD 650, before the Chinese influence had radiated this far. The first scrolls discovered here were written in Sanskrit-Brahmi, about the sciences of medicine and necromancy. Two gigantic Buddhas had once flanked the road. But I found only an old town wall and a fallen watchtower. Nowadays Kucha seems to specialise in producing bricks; I wandered past rows of kilns in working order, and rows of ruined ones, fallen down.

After stopping at a shack café for a cup of tea, I refilled my flask from the teapot and gave the empty pot back to the proprietor, with some money to cover the cost. He gave me too much change (tea costs one fen – ½p) so I left 10 fen on the table (to cover the flaskful). As I re-boarded the bus the man came running up indignantly giving back the 10 fen and telling me I'd paid for the tea and the extra was free with his compliments. It illustrated the manners and honesty of many people I had encountered and I knew that I was safe among them.

After leaving Kucha, the road links a string of oases which are sustained by a series of shallow lakes. Most of these oases are modern Chinese industrial townships, producing building materials. That is one thing which abounds in the desert. Standing in the barrenness we would see small groups of people sieving sand and gravel; they wore dust-masks. It looked to me like a grim way to earn a living, and a fellow passenger said that the people were a labour force of political dissidents from the south.

Some older oases are known for other products in which they have specialised for countless generations: whetstone for grinding knives, inkstone for calligraphists, axle-grease, fine sand for polishing jade, and gold dust. Marco Polo mentions mines producing steel and zinc but it was the asbestos which fascinated him because it can be put into a fire but will not burn: 'A fossil substance with fibres not unlike those of wool. When woven into cloth and thrown into the fire it remains incombustible.' He calls it salamander, and notes that in Rome there was a napkin woven from this material, sent as a gift from one of the Tartar Princes to the Roman Pontiff. One hopes it didn't damage his health too much.

From a low series of rocky hills we went down into a gravelly grey-brown basin. In the sky to the north were glimpses of tall white mountains, while the south grew very flat. Far-distant green oases were marked out by hardy poplar trees; roadside patches of irrigation produced fields of wheat, and the wasteland was planted with water melons. The air here was so clear that we could see for many miles. But there was nothing to watch or look at, nothing happening. No singing from the baritone – he must have fallen asleep.

Somewhere in that flatness is the deep gorge of the Tarim River, flowing east. I was particularly interested in the rivers I came across as the bulkiest item in my backpack was my inflatable canoe. It rolls up to the size of a sleeping bag, and its paddle unscrews into four parts, making the whole thing invisible in my backpack. Canoeing is an enjoyable way to travel and I hoped it could take me where roads could not. I had paddled a dugout a thousand miles down the Congo, and spent four months exploring the tributaries of the Sepik River in Papua New Guinea. Later I had also had my introduction to shooting rapids in Papua New Guinea, rafting down the Wahgi, one of the fiercest white water rivers in the world. It had given me a taste for more.

From what I'd heard of the Tarim it didn't sound right for me and my canoe because of its 200-feet sheer cliffs with no view of the desert. But in 1899 the Swedish scientist geographer Sven Hedin made an expedition through this desert in a locally made boat in order to map the Yarkand and Tarim Rivers. He voyaged for eighty days and his luggage included a musical box on which he played tunes from *Carmen* and the Swedish national anthem. I wondered how soon I would find a good river for my canoe.

After driving for ten hours we stopped for the night at a truckers' yard in a rather swampy oasis whose mosquitoes were fat and plentiful. My dormitory on the second night was crowded with five beds, my women room-mates were two Han Chinese and two Uighurs with children who shared their beds. The atmosphere was strained. Clearly the two groups have little in common; by nature the Uighur tend to be pleasure-loving, restless and impetuous. The Han are conscientious, methodical and conventional. They like to think things out in advance. Their present mastery over Xinjiang is nothing new; they first conquered it about 100 BC. As a border province Xinjiang has long been a politically turbulent area. In 1931, after a Moslem rising against extortionate taxation, 200,000 people were killed, and the Han governor closed the border to stop news of the massacre getting out. My Uighur room-mates were en route to Aksu, where the last bloody uprising took place in 1980–1.

The third morning of our journey was grey with a howling wind that blotted out the view. Some ruined watchtowers lay near the road. They had been tall structures, part of a defensive chain. Even their stumps stood high above the land, but now in ruins; they were being absorbed back into the desert. Other hummocks which puzzled me were many conical windswept mounds on an otherwise flat plain. To ask my fellow passengers what they signified I took a paper and pencil, drew a mound and put a questioning expression on my face. My neighbour shook her head and passed the paper to someone else. He drew a picture of a tree, and more trees, until it dawned on me that I was seeing the remains of what had long ago been a forest. Suddenly I remembered reading that early travellers had spoken of great forests and others mentioned finding massive stumps of trees whose roots had been exposed by eroding sand levels. In a small oasis I saw bundles of roots stacked up, as firewood, for sale to passing truck-drivers.

Winter in these regions would be very cold, the temperature can drop well below freezing, while the summer Gobi temperature reaches 120°F in the shade. Yet now in May it was still cold first thing; I wore a woolly cardigan, and adopted the local women's tradition of wearing a skirt over trousers. By midday the air was warmer and there were frequent dust-storms. On a detour around an impassable section of road we went a few

miles, then the bus-driver stopped and began scanning the
horizons, clearly lost. To all sides were the hummocky remains
of a forest. A couple of men climbed on to the roof to look for
tracks and after an hour of trial and error we found the route
again.

At a couple of small oases we halted to have lunch, or drink
tea and refill our water bottles. Playing cards is a favourite oasis
pastime, and gambling used to be compulsive, but it was made
illegal. So was mahjong. In many oases some of the dwellings
are built underground, as protection from the summer heat and
the howling, gritty winds. These hut-sized rectangular pits are
reached by a sloping trench and roofed over with wood, poles,
straw matting and a layer of sand – making them invisible but
for the occasional chimneys sticking up through the sand.

Back inside the bus, I brought out my map of China to see
how far we had progressed, and people crowded around to
take a look. I was impressed by how many of them knew how
to read a map. To make use of my companions' interest I asked
various people to show me their home town. Some came from
distant places and when I asked them their reasons for making
this bus journey one said, 'Because we are moving house. We've
been re-allocated to work in Xinjiang.' On further questioning I
learned that they hated the idea but the Party does not give
them any choice. In order to stabilise minority areas, the Chinese
have used compulsory transmigration schemes to implant Han
Chinese throughout the territory, sending the unfortunate
chosen families to live away from their own culture and friends
in a barren desert land of Moslems. Many migrants will never
return home except for brief visits, even though it may be their
wish to do so.

The plain we crossed in the late afternoon had glittering white
salt flats and its root-hummocks were covered in dry green
desert plants. Our night stop was a walled oasis with no
greenery, just a couple of well shafts and some heaps of chalky
white stone which the local peasants had been firing in underground kilns. Wisps of pale smoke drifted up and out into the
evening sky. I sat near a well and watched people coming to
fill their makeshift pairs of buckets slung on shoulder poles.
The water was forty feet below ground. A crowd gathered to
stare at me and block my view. Some children took me to their
home for a cup of hot water. Hot water is commonly drunk
instead of tea.

As usual I slept in a women's dormitory at the local inn.

Dust-storms in the night blew in through the cracks in the door and by morning my face, hair and bed were coated in grit. The morning brought desert pink sand and mud mountains eroded into alluvial fan patterns, red at their base. The bus trundled on slowly and at every slight slope the driver shifted gear into neutral so we freewheeled along at ten miles an hour. It was becoming a little boring, so I was pleased when on our fourth day we arrived in Kashgar and my frustration was replaced by joy at having reached the crossroads of Asia.

3 The crossroads of Asia

The streets and alleyways of Kashgar were alive with a blend of Eastern and nomadic cultures; tall, hook-nosed men with high cheekbones and long beards, prayer caps, turbans and Cossack-style fur hats; some of the women's faces were veiled by thick brown shawls like large tablecloths. When a woman is veiled I can't tell which way she's facing unless she's walking along, or standing gossiping in a gaggle.

Because there are no westernised maps of Kashgar city I set out from my hotel the next morning on a rented bicycle, intending to draw a sketch map and to learn my way around. The Post Office was my first stop because I wanted to post mail home. Outside it sat the professional letter-writer. His clients were three women veiled in brown; he listened to what they wanted to say then began to write, no doubt in the appropriate flowery tone. His skill as a master of words is important because, writing in Arabic, one simple root word can be built up to give it many shades of meaning. This scribe didn't know how to write in Chinese – probably there was no demand for it.

A British Consulate, and a Russian one, had existed in Kashgar until about 1947. I cycled past the British one, last occupied by the famous climber and explorer, Eric Shipton. It's now a distinctly shabby boarding house for truck-drivers and merchants. In the main square some men sat under shady trees strumming traditional guitars. An assortment of cripples also came through on their way to the central mosque. All around this area the alleys are warren-like and have open-fronted workshops and market kiosks, each only about ten feet square. From the bright sunshine in the street I peered into many dim kiosks to see their crafts. One lane contained carpenters whose lathes are turned by hand, using a long looped string attached to a stick. One hand pulls the stick to and fro to rotate the lathe, the other holds a sharp chisel to carve rings and grooves into wooden knobs and legs. Blacksmiths were making plough-shares. A man held a sheet of red-hot metal with two pairs of pincers while his partner, wielding a three-foot hammer, combined rhythm and muscles to beat it flat. Others hammered tin to make buckets and bowls, producing an alleyful of rapping, tapping noises. The repairing of burned-out kettles is good business here. And grinding-stones the size of mill-wheels were being chipped into shape. Splinters of rock came flying across the dusty road. Knife-grinders plied their trade using round local whetstones turned by attachment to a bicycle wheel and pedals.

The roads were busy with bicycles and donkey carts. Cart drivers called out to their donkeys using clicks, clucks and guttural sounds to convey their commands. The command for reverse is a brrr noise, and they purr with pursed lips to steady the animal. Uighur speech also has many abrupt sounds and word-endings like *-isk, -isch,* and *-ske.*

On a bridge sat some beggars – not a normal sight in China nowadays, though in the past they were about as plentiful as in India. The Chinese government had a clean-up campaign and swept them off the streets, because the presence of beggars can be interpreted as showing that communism does not meet everyone's needs. The beggars held dishes of dry crumbs, symbolising their poverty. One blind boy was playing a lute and singing. Many people paused to give them loose change.

Beneath shady trees barbers were at work shaving men's heads. The long moustaches are treated with gel and beards are combed to a point. Beyond them were sellers of silks, cottons, gaudy materials and scarves, and then food: meat kebabs, honey, nuts and dried fruit. I indulged in a slab of toffee-coated walnuts. It gave power to my pedalling.

The public security bureau was on my list of places to find, in order to apply for a special permit. When I located it I parked my bicycle at the end of a row of policemen's bikes. Unfortunately my bike fell over and hit the bike next to it, which hit another and another; I watched with dismay as slowly the motion rippled along knocking every bike flat into the dust. I didn't get my permit. Decided to try again the following day. On my way back to the hotel the sky ahead went yellow and minutes later the air was thick with dust that swirled violently in every direction; the wind roared, and when I glanced ahead I couldn't see a thing, and my eyelashes became matted with grit.

The next morning I went by bike to buy fresh hot bread (crusty and unleavened) for breakfast but the baker I'd found the previous day only had cold bread so I refused to buy any. After cycling around town I still hadn't found any hot bread and, not wanting to lose face by going back to a baker I'd refused I dived down a side avenue. There I noticed the smell of fresh bread coming from a small clay oven; the baker was just opening for business, and to go with the bread I picked a few ripe mulberries from the trees outside his shop.

In the shade of the trees two blacksmiths were shoeing mules. This interested me because I'm an amateur at shoeing. To prevent the mules from kicking they used their traditional blacksmith's sling, which is a raised ridge pole with two ropes around the mule's girth and haunches so its weight is suspended and it cannot run anywhere. One back leg is tied to the back support pole and to stop a mule from biting the smiths tie its halter tightly to the front support. When it's neatly trussed up, the smith gets on with fitting the thin shoes and cutting the hooves to match; nails in and twist, cut and hammer it smooth, quick and dexterous, the same as my local blacksmith in England.

In the evening I went for a bike ride outside the town and got lost in the wheatfields as twilight faded into darkness. The bike had no lights. Even when I found wide paths to ride along I was unnerved to meet donkey carts bowling along at a smart trot. When I'd had enough of being lost I stopped a donkey cart which was going to town, put my bicycle on the cart and accepted a lift. The old man even let me drive the donkey.

The only disappointing thing about Kashgar is how little there is for the average tourist to go and look at. There were quite a lot of overseas travellers in Kashgar, coming from many parts of the world, particularly Australia, Scandinavia, USA and England. The majority were intelligent and thoughtful people, travelling in small groups, and some had come alone; most only stayed for three or four days. The places to visit in Kashgar are not spectacular because they're made of mud and straw, which doesn't last long, though one building outside the town is a magnificent exception. It houses the tombs of the Abakhajias (Holy Men of Islam). I cycled there; it was not too far but the road was terribly stony. The tombs are set in a domed mausoleum, like a small Taj Mahal at the back of a village. The walled garden is devotedly maintained to keep it in flower with different plants throughout the year, edged by mosaic paths with strips of decorative tiles, and the air is murmurous with pigeons. The outer gate-tower, tiled in blue and white patterns, stands by an open-air mosque decorated with painted murals of mountain scenes, lakes and birds. The mausoleum itself is a massive green-tiled building with central dome and four minarets whose turrets of wooden latticework have smaller painted domes. The main doors were locked but the curator was fetched to let me in. It was suddenly cool after the fierce heat outside. I was led into a dark corridor and couldn't see a thing. The curator's voice echoed back and I realised that he'd turned a corner, then I saw light ahead and emerged into the inner hall. Fifty-eight tombs sat on a large dais. These include the tombs of five Abakhajias plus their families and other wise men. In the last corner is an ornate wooden hearse (hand carried) with a coffin inscribed and painted with insignias and painted silver insets. The curator tried to explain it all in Uighur; of course I didn't understand a word but marvelled at the magnificent echoes produced by his voice beneath the dome.

As I cycled back towards town I detoured to avoid a stony section of road, and took to the paths through the fields. This was how I came across a vast old Moslem cemetery, mile upon mile of crumbling vaults, made of clay and straw, shaped like long domed coffins or else circular resembling bee-hives. Many vaults had fallen inwards revealing dark holes underground. Occasionally the ground beneath me was so thin I could feel it sink under my weight. Through low mud walls and archways filtered birdsong and the distant barking of dogs, I could also hear the murmuring dirge of three old men in turbans sitting by a family grave. Further on, a party of grave-diggers showed me a separate walled area with a special kind of dome, now almost in ruins. I wondered if it would be where the holy men used to shut themselves away alone for forty days without food. A jug of water would be given to them each day but no other contact was made. I sat in the dome for a moment, thinking about those long vigils of prayer.

Not all the graves were old. The straw chaff in newly made tombs reflected the sun like flecks of gold. The saddest graves were the tiny ones of infants. As I left a funeral procession came along the track. The rib-frame coffin and cloth-wrapped corpse were carried by a party of men and the whole procession was wailing with sorrow. At the full moon there would be a festival of the dead. It is held at every important mosque and entails much chanting, and banging of gongs and cymbals all night.

At another local celebration an American photo-journalist caused problems by taking eight of his foreign friends, each being snap-happy with cameras, and proving too much of a strain on the party, who finally asked them to leave. But I had the story at secondhand. At first hand, the day I spent in his company ended with him having to write an official self-criticism of his behaviour to the security police. It started when he hired one of the few cars in town to take us sightseeing outside town. Unfortunately, although the tourist board mention ancient caves and ruins, they're not worth visiting. But in the desert on the way back we passed a halted convoy of prison buses. The prisoners, guarded by a square of armed soldiers, were squatting in groups on the ground. The American whipped out his camera and took photos as we drove slowly past. The folly of such an action should be apparent to anyone who has spent time in the Third World or touchy countries. I don't know how the security police discovered it was he but when they visited him they confiscated all his film. This, for a photo-journalist, is unlucky. He was also unlucky to have an arrogant nature, a showy temper and enough fluency in Mandarin to be able to insult the Chinese to their faces. I thought it was surprisingly tolerant of the authorities to be content with the films, plus a fine of 40 yuan (about £13) and a written self-criticism. He was asked to re-write the self-criticism five times before it was approved as sufficiently humble.

Sunday is bazaar day in Kashgar. Among travellers, this market is reputed to rank as one of the world's most fascinating, along with Fez and Kano in Africa. The road leading into the bazaar was jammed solid with donkey carts; several had managed to get in a tangle, one pulling a load of two thirty-foot poplar tree trunks had got hooked into a cart coming in the opposite direction. In every space were people pushing bicycles, ringing their bike bells, while the donkey cart drivers yelled a word that sounded like 'Push! Push!' The donkey cart parking-lot stretched right back to a stream; lines of carts with shafts pointing skywards and lines of donkeys tied opposite them, each with his own small supply of fresh lucerne and chopped straw to eat. Angry donkeys snorted and brayed at each other.

The most entertaining section is the livestock market. At one side of it I found tethered lines of camels. They looked rather motheaten because their winter coats were shedding, hanging off in thick wadges. Few had fat humps, but their prices seemed reasonable: 400 yuan (£132) for a baby camel, 600 for an average adult and 800 yuan for a good-looking one. There were many ponies for sale, and potential buyers were trying them out, galloping up and down the livestock area dodging animals and seeing how quickly they could stop. A good horse is worth

800–1,000 yuan. Groups of men sat and argued over prices, and when a deal was concluded they shook hands solemnly, binding the bargain. The cattle were being pinched and prodded by people wanting to find out how much flesh they had. With sheep, one feels for the fatness of the tail flaps. Tails are not cropped and much of the animal's fatty goodness is stored in the tail and haunch flaps. Innumerable donkeys and goats completed the scene and the only irritation was the crowd of staring people that surrounded me whenever I sat down. Since the day was growing hotter I retreated to the fleece and wool market for a cup of cold tea, and didn't realise until too late that the tea was made from water in the market ditch, but hoped my stomach wouldn't suffer the consequences. Traders were haggling over piles of semi-cured fleeces and sacks of wool shearings, some of it cashmere. It's said that an experienced wool trader can tell in what terrain the sheep and goats have been grazing by the feel of the wool. Woollen rugs and traditional Kashgar carpets were on display in other areas, and bright cloths being examined by the brown-veiled women. Men's hat-makers were offering fur-lined hats trimmed with leopard, bear and wolf. And there were boot-makers, leather-workers, tack-makers, people selling wooden pitchforks made from peeled branches; and rope-makers, knife-traders, vendors of photos of oriental pop stars, and boys with baskets going around collecting donkey dung to dry for fuel.

Exhausted, I retired from the throng and spent a quiet afternoon talking to a local herbalist whose wares were on show in a side street. The herbalist was quite happy for me to investigate his potions and tell me their uses. Dried snake is for chest pains, though for a cough remedy he recommends dried lizards mixed with some green pellets. Powdered armadillo is given for relief of morning sickness, while for a stomach complaint he would supply elkhorn. He had racks of snake-skins, pungent smelling roots (snake venom antidote), tortoiseshell, sea porcupines, and bats pinned up with their wings outstretched. Also dried birds' heads, mushrooms, bottles of leaves, and slimy-looking things in oil; I tried some freshly-ground rose petals mixed with sugar which the herbalist assured me would be a tonic and keep me fit and strong.

4   A canoe on Lake Karakol

Marco Polo, together with his father and uncle, had reached Kashgar in 1273. This was the second time that his father and uncle had come to China. Their first journey there had happened by chance because they got detoured on a trade-expedition and ended up near the Black Sea. War broke out and made their return to Venice impractical, so they went east, reaching Persia and the Tartar kingdoms, where they met an ambassador of the Chinese emperor. He persuaded them to go with him to China and meet the emperor, the great Kublai Khan, one of the mightiest of all earthly kings. At the end of that first journey, when the Polo brothers took their leave, the Khan asked them to carry a message to the Pope in Rome, requesting the Pope to send him some Christian missionaries and some holy oil. The Polos returned to Venice, and set out for China the second time in 1271, taking with them Marco, who was then seventeen years old.

This journey took three and a half years, one way. The few missionaries sent by the Pope deserted on route, but the Polos carried the holy oil, and didn't seem unduly concerned about having lost the missionaries. Whether they knew the import-ance of the link they were reviving between west and east, or just travelled for its own sake, I'm not sure. As they approached Kashgar on the Silk Road over the Pamir Mountains, Marco Polo describes a fifty-day march among elevated peaks and plains, and 'ascending mountain after mountain until the sur-rounding summits seemed to be the highest lands in the world'. He noted that at high altitude our food does not cook as quickly or fires give the same heat as down in the lowlands; which, as all modern high-altitude travellers know, is a fact of life. But in the Polos' day it was an unknown phenomenon.

The Pamirs were later crossed by explorers and geographers of the eighteenth and nineteenth centuries, and by some of the archaeologists, now regarded as robbers, who came in search of the lost cities of the Taklamakan Basin. The bulk of the Pamir Range is in Russia but its eastern portion in China contains two mountains of outstanding size, Mustagh Ata (24,758ft/7546m) and Kongur (25,324ft/7719m). There is a road leading up into these Chinese Pamirs, which links China with Pakistan, an international frontier not open nowadays to foreigners. The idea of spending a few days travelling up that way was tempting. So I renewed my effort to get a special permit for it. Success, and at the same time a young Dutchman called Peter was also granted a permit, so we decided to hitch together.

At 5 a.m. the next morning we set out. Peter made some rude comments about the weight of my backpack. I didn't tell him that there was a canoe in it. We flagged several trucks before one stopped for us. It was carrying a load of bricks. The driver was a young Han and in reply to my question *'Ni dao shenme difang chiu?'* (You to what place go?), he said that he was going all the way to the Pakistan border. We hopped in and I sat in the middle since Peter couldn't speak Mandarin. I enjoyed practising and the driver didn't mind my mistakes. He said that the border was about 200 miles away, and he would reach it on the following day. Actually I had no intention of going that far, I just wanted to ramble in the Chinese Pamirs.

After passing out of the city limits we crossed the fertile plain of wheat plots and poplar trees and two hours later came out into a desert landscape of stony sand and wind-moulded dunes in parallel lines. Ahead lay a crumpled complex of red hills, very weathered and backed by immense, snowy mountain peaks. This was where we were heading. The road was dirt, corrugated by truck tyres but a much better-made surface than I had expected. We began a long slow climb up a broad valley, beside a small river. It was small in this season, but the width of its boulder strewn bed told me that it can grow into a large torrent when summer comes to the Pamirs and the snows melt. Over the next few hours as we climbed we often saw the river in the gorge below the road, and I looked at it in terms of being runnable by canoe. It was rapid in parts but looked feasible. To the east the Pamirs merge with the Kunlun Range which divides the Tibetan highlands from the desert of Taklamakan. Kunlun means Mountains of Darkness.

At the first security roadblock we were stopped by a pole-barrier across the road. Peter and I were escorted into a dilapidated shack, the office, where we showed our permits. The checkpoint was probably because we were coming close to the Russian border. The other traffic was a few trucks, army jeeps and occasional horsemen wearing woolly hats with earflaps, riding long-maned and fiery ponies, and there was a road-grader being drawn by a camel.

By noon we were up around the base of Mount Kongur, which towered up and was lost in clouds. The road goes on past Kongur and there was a truckers' inn where we had lunch of noodles and soup. The next major mountain is Mustagh Ata, which we also skirted, passing little Lake Karakol and getting good backward views of the main Lake Karakol lying between Kongur and Mustagh Ata; a vibrantly blue lake fed by gigantic glaciers coming down from slopes hidden by heavy cloud. Peter was keen to see how far we could go along the road, and I let him persuade me not to leave the truck just yet. On our way up the pass after Mustagh Ata we got hit by a snow-storm. Visibility outside was nearly nil and snowflakes blew in through the door frames. The cold was intense. My rucksack on the back of the truck was getting soaked in snow, so I brought it into the cab and we sat with it across our knees. It was like holding a solid block of ice.

At another security roadblock we again showed our permits. I had doubts that we should have come this far but I couldn't read the Chinese characters written on the permits. Actually I don't think that the security guards at the checkpoints could read Chinese either, because they looked at the permits and let us through. According to my map we were now moving along parallel to the Russian border, going south toward Pakistan and Afghanistan which are about eighty miles away from here. On the pass, the weather changed and we emerged into dusty sunshine. It felt like being on the top of the world; its lunar scenery was bare and barren. Sharks' teeth mountains stretched in long ridges, capped in snow and ice. We passed a small caravan of five laden camels, roped in a line with youngsters roaming free. Small baby camels are sometimes carried in a wooden basket on their mothers' backs.

Gradually the road descended into a broad grassy valley, and at the small town of Taxkorgan we stopped for the night. It was 7 p.m. and there were still three more hours of daylight left so Peter and I put our baggage at an inn and went to explore the town. The truck-driver went to join some of his cronies at another inn. The town centre was dull and crowds of people gathered to stare at us; the people are tall and carry themselves well; their faces were narrow and handsome. But I noticed some surly, suspicious stares, and even had the uncomfortable impression that we were being followed. So we twisted and turned through the back lanes until we had lost any escort, then went for a walk along the edge of town. Here we met a man whose sincere smile persuaded us to stop and make friends. A Tajik tribesman, but he could speak four languages: Pakistani, Tajik, Khirgiz and Uighur, and we communicated in signals and common nouns. Peter had a repertoire of grunts which he uses instead of words, making sentences from lines of grunts illustrated by pantomime. When I asked the man how many different animals he owned, Peter supplied the animal noises, enabling me to discover that our new friend was the wealthy owner of four camels, two horses and thirty sheep. He called his sheep to him before dark, and they came running from the plain, and flocked around his small stone house, clearly waiting to be let inside. He explained that he usually feeds his sheep in the evening and they do sleep in the house. He said that there are wolves and wild sheep in the mountains. Marco Polo had also mentioned wild sheep, large ones whose horns were up to six palms in length. According to later travellers, they were probably a species of ibex or mountain goat.

The man's wife and two daughters arrived back from an outing and we all went into the house to drink tea. From the outside it was a stone shack; but inside was warm and homely. The outer room was a swept earth kitchen and animal area, and it led into the family room, richly carpeted on floors and walls with red and blue traditional rugs. The lounging and sleeping area was a raised platform occupying most of the room. Its inside was made of clay or stones and heated in winter by flues from the kitchen stove. What a sensible idea. We drank tea from porcelain cups and listened to Radio Pakistan by lamplight. My picture postcards were passed around and the family wouldn't let us leave until after supper, which was deliciously tender hunks of steamed mutton. Later in the evening our host took us to visit some of his friends, and among them was an old man who played a flute made from the hollow wing-bone of a big bird.

The next morning Peter went out for an early walk and although I looked for him in town, I couldn't find him. How can one lose a man who's head and shoulders taller than anyone in town, with blond hair? So, assuming that we would meet up again later I decided to borrow a horse and spend the morning having a ride. It wasn't that easy to borrow a horse. The horses are not gentle and men didn't think I could handle one. Perhaps they also didn't trust me to bring it back. Finally I prevailed and was loaned a little grey stallion. It was fun to ride, fast and able to turn quickly; I chose a direction away from the borders so that no one would get the wrong idea, and went across the valley to the east. All around were snow-capped mountains. It felt good to be in the saddle again. Under its saddle the horse wore a wool blanket which covered its back, as did many of the other horses being galloped on their morning's errands. Without these rugs their sweat would cause chills in the icy wind. My steed's hooves thudded gently over the dried-up marshland grass and moss which held tiny yellow and blue flowers. As grazing goes, the grass was short-cropped and it would be hard work for any animal to eat his fill, yet all over the plain I could see herds of grazing cattle, horses and sheep. The air was silent except for bursts of distant braying and neighing, birdsong and the occasional frog.

People were scarce; there were a few out tending their herds but when I approached them they ran away. I took the horse back to his owner and set off on foot to try and meet some of them. The reds and silvers of women's clothes stood out from afar, but perhaps the fairness of my hair also stood out and the people simply kept their distance, retreating whenever I approached. The women who sat outside their crofts went inside and barred their doorways. A couple of young girls that I caught by surprise screamed in terror and one burst into tears before they ran away. So I began walking sideways and stalking people as one would stalk a timid animal. When fairly close to some women I greeted them in Tajik and held out a brightly coloured postcard to show them. Their faces were a study of fear versus curiosity, so going a bit closer I put the card on the ground and went back to a safe distance. One woman wavered then came and took the card back to the group. With the second picture I didn't let go until near enough to hand it to them, and explained to them that it was a photo of my parents. I think the importance of this picture is that suddenly you are no longer just a foreign devil, you are also a person with a mother and father, like anyone else.

Finally I sat down on a dry mossy bank and the women sat and crouched beside me. Their long black plaits were decorated and beaded with buttons. Some women had five or six plaits; they also wore scarves and necklaces of red and coral beads, and earrings of other beads and coral. To keep warm they wore padded jackets padded with horsehair and wool, worn over waisted dresses, baggy trousers, and red leather boots with toes curling upwards. The babies carried by some women had extra padded cloth bootees and helmets. One child was crying and its mother sang a lullaby. When she finished she asked me to sing one of my country's lullabies, which I did and they all seemed to enjoy it. Gradually they accepted me.

Their houses are crofts made of pebbles and mud, or brick-like sods of turf. Heaps of brush and root firewood for fuel are augmented by dry animal dung, which is gathered and put to dry in the sun. Some women were at work making braided ropes, others came to exchange greetings. Their salutation was the touching of cheeks, or kissing each other's cheeks. One man greeted some women by kissing their hands. It all seemed very French to me. I asked about bride-price and was told that a good local woman is worth ten sheep, a cow, and about one thousand yuan. I doubt many men can afford more than one wife.

After I found Peter later that day we left Taxkorgan, and chanced to get a lift back north with the same obliging Han truck-driver who had brought us from Kashgar, making his return trip. At the base of Mustagh Ata we parted from the truck and walked to Subush, a hamlet of fortress-type buildings set on raised mounds in the flat basin. It was snowing so we spent the night there. My objective now was Lake Karakol, the blue lake created by the thick glaciers melting off Mustagh Ata. I wanted to follow in the wake of Sven Hedin, who had paddled across it surveying the area in 1894. I hoped to fare better, however, as he had nearly drowned.

Before dawn we set off for the lakeshore, and Peter helped me to inflate my canoe but said it looked unstable and went off for a stroll. The ice in the shallows cracked easily as I jabbed my paddle into it. Dawn broke first over Mustagh Ata, casting a golden glow on to its whiteness. The water mirrored the land's jagged peaks. Ripples from my progress picked up the light's reflections and sent them outward as fat daggers of light wafting across the glassy lake. I pushed my paddle vertically downwards and it hit the lake bottom, which was reassuring. The danger was from storms and Hedin describes 'hurricane-like squalls from the south sweeping over the lake, ploughing up the water furiously'. The altitude was probably about 11,800 feet. As the wind gusted the lake became choppy and I was bitterly cold despite wearing every piece of clothing I'd got, plus using my sheet-liner wrapper around my head as a scarf. Peter was standing on the shore flapping his arms to keep warm. Later he and I parted company; he had a time limit and needed to hurry to Beijing.

I came back to the lake. My canoe rippled and splashed as it ran before the wind, I paddled but let the wind push us wherever it was going. Sven Hedin's boat had been an inflatable of a sort, made from some inflated goatskins attached to yurt poles and the hide of a horse which had conveniently died. The oars were made from poles split at one end with a piece of goatskin stretched across the fork. For a rudder Hedin used his spade, and the sail was of local red cotton. His boat was only slightly bigger than mine, both being about six feet long but his was three feet wide, more of a coracle than a canoe. He described his boat 'as warped and angular as an empty sardine box'. He added: 'As our brave craft, in which I was going to navigate the Karakol for a whole week, lay bobbing up and down near the shore on her inflated goat-skins, she put me strongly in mind of some unknown antediluvian creature hatching its eggs'. The local Kirghiz didn't use boats and had been astounded, as well they might be, by Hedin's, for they had not even been able to imagine the idea of a boat. 'But,' he said, 'it is doubtful if it impressed them with any admiration of my national Swedish navigation.' On his first sounding expedition a passing squall hit the lake, the goat-skin bags began to come adrift and collapse with a hissing of air, while every wave broke into the boat. But he reached the shore and tried again the next day.

My canoe, a French Sevylor craft, is infinitely more stream-lined and easily manoeuvrable, though I had to stop and collect a rock to hold down the nose. When its nose is too lightweight it doesn't steer well. Just for demonstration I paddled some tight figures of eight, though there was no one to be impressed, and raced myself from one side to the other. I liked the way that the turquoise colour of the water changed according to depth and to the state of the sky, which suddenly clouded over then came clear again. But Mustagh Ata was left engulfed, making its own clouds. Sven Hedin made several attempts to climb the mountain, but his best effort took him 3000 feet below the summit. Eric Shipton got to within 200 feet with Tilman in 1947, while he was British Consul General in Kashgar. For a while I watched and pondered Mustagh Ata's misty bulk, then turned and paddled back to the northern end to look for an exit stream leading towards Mount Kongur.

The river flowed out beneath moraine so I carried the canoe until it became navigable. It coursed along a grassy valley and was split into several channels. My paddle hit the gravel bed sometimes and on turning shallow corners we bounced over pebbles. When I lifted my head I saw that all around were minor snowy peaks sloping down through barren sweeps into grassy valleys. Two tributaries swelled my stream, one from little Lake Karakol, and the larger from the glacier fields of Mustagh Ata and Kongur. Mount Kongur didn't seem to have any obvious peak; it is a hulking lumpy plateau with several summits jutting above its dark shield of ice-veined rock.

In 1980 the renowned climber Chris Bonington got permission to climb Mount Kongur, at the time the highest unclimbed peak in China. But Kongur proved a difficult challenge, made hazardous by avalanches and hidden crevasses, and near the top a storm forced his team to dig 'snow-coffins' in which they lay for three days and nights while the storm raged outside, before they reached the summit. The shape of a mountain can be as individual as a person's face, first seen as a distant two-dimensional image which looms up as it is approached, then vanishing and coming back into sight as one meanders through its buttressing ridges and forked valleys. Mountains have a multi-faceted nature that is gradually revealed by observation from different points. Each point of view brings new understanding. Longer communing with a mountain brings a special significance. Later when the mountain recedes into the distance, it will be recognisable even as an undistinguished peak in a horizon of mountains.

A snow-storm blew up. Seeing some huts not far from the river, I went to seek shelter and was offered a cup of tea by the Kirghiz family living there. The tea was brewed with sheep's milk and the stove was fuelled by dried sheep's dropping. From the stove the woman took a freshly-baked bread-cake; it was delicious. The man of the house was ill, he had a fever but he had been seen and treated by a doctor. I spent a short time in conversation with him. He was not a poor man, he owned twenty-five sheep, two horses, some yaks and two camels. Near his stone and mud hut was a round felt yurt; the children said their grandmother lived there, and took me to meet her. From behind the heavy felt curtain, which acted as a front door, there was strung a mysterious long woven strip of material which stretched some way outside and its end was pegged to the ground.

We called out and the children pushed aside the curtain for me to enter. The yurt's interior was spacious, warm from the stove and thick felt walls, and airy because of a large circular opening in the roof. The old lady was working at a tripod-shaped loom, nimbly weaving more of the long woollen strip in a blend of red, yellow and green. A calf and a baby goat were resting in a section partitioned off for them.

When the storm abated I said my goodbyes, collected the canoe which I had tied to the yurt, and returned to the river which followed Kongur's base for about two miles and gathered water from three glaciers. The vast size of the mountain filled the whole of my eastern horizon. It made me feel as insignificant as an ant or a particle of sand. The watercourse flowed through an area of prickly scrub, less than a yard tall but spikier than a coil of barbed wire. I wondered if it is the type of sand millet whose seeds can be made into flour, and maybe baked into the type of cake that I'd just eaten. People don't try to touch the spiky bush, they just put a cloth underneath and hit it with sticks until the grains fall.

Still meandering in many shallow channels, I grated over pebbles a couple of times and nearly got snagged on some prickly branches which had fallen into the water. Later I did notice that a little air was escaping from one tube of the canoe but it could only have been a pinprick and it stayed afloat well enough. As I approached a U-bend the current began pushing the canoe too close to a bank overhung with prickles. I steered away but the current steered more strongly. With growing alarm I directed the canoe across the river, straining to get away from the bank. The canoe suddenly responded, shooting us into the shallows, now broadside to the stream. Trying to swing the nose straight I hit a rock, the canoe bounced off it and straightened up backwards. Now facing the wrong way, I looked over my shoulder and realised that the river was growing quickly narrower. For some harrowing moments I paddled cautiously, twisting around to see what we were in for. Another bend loomed, I couldn't manage it in reverse, the movements are back to front. My confidence plummeted and I misjudged it. We hit a sandy piece of cliff which crumbled down on to the spraydeck cover, but in that moment I had space to spin the nose downriver. Awkwardly achieved, but at least I was now facing forward again.

From Kongur's base the river descended into barren scenery, under an iron roadbridge and down a deceptively swift stretch where the water looked a milky blue colour. The weather began to get worse, there was strong wind and a few snowflakes. I hurried for several miles until the clouds cleared away to the south, leaving me in an area of silvery white sand mountains, their shape eroded into flowing curves which glistened in the cold sunlight. The beauty there was something special. Perhaps it was enhanced by being so little known and untraversed. The river spread again into a series of ponds; a marshland of sedge-tussocks. The chains of pools grew so shallow that I portaged around them and put in again where the river became deep. It was at the beginning of a gorge. Its barren sides grew taller and its course was made rough by boulders, but there was nothing threatening and I thoroughly enjoyed learning to handle my canoe. So far I had stayed fairly dry, the spraydeck covers at front and back were effective and my small bag of luggage was tucked down by my legs. Steering and driving the canoe with a double-bladed paddle is certainly simpler than using a wooden one-bladed type.

Another blizzard blew up and since it was late in the day I stopped as soon as I found a hut where I could shelter. It was a cold but uneventful night, and the next day began with that crystal sunshine you only find at high altitudes. The air was as crisp and pure as the cry of a falcon. By mid-morning I'd gone through a section of brown shale mountains, seeming bleached of all colour. Bare rock, sometimes banded with whites and reds, and no plants except sparse spiky brush. And beyond it all, the icy peaks and glaciers.

The river grew steeper but because it wasn't in flood, it poured evenly over ledges and down over boulder obstacles in fairly gentle chutes. The canoe bucked its way through them, but at one chute I hit a boulder at the wrong angle. Suddenly we tipped sideways. I shoved my paddle-blade against another rock to push myself upright, the blade slipped and, dropping the paddle I reached out to fend us off by hand. It worked, but the paddle was gone. Anxiously scanning the water I saw it nearby and managed to paddle with my hands and retrieve it. Fortunately at this point the river was not fast, and although there were some long, semi-turbulent stretches, they looked rougher than they really were. At one of the quieter pools I stopped to have a short rest and munch on some of the dried food that I still carried. It was rather idyllic. I doubted that the river had ever been run before, since for most of the year it's swollen and totally unnavigable. But being the first wasn't important, I wasn't trying to achieve anything. I just wanted to try out my canoe. The voyage wouldn't be a long one, just a day or so, since the river's lower course near Kashgar, which goes through endless flat wheat fields, didn't interest me.

Some tribesmen on horseback caught sight of me, their horses muffled up in blankets and the men in woolly coats and hats. One was carrying a baby yak across his saddle. I waved but they had already spurred their steeds and were hurrying away along the track halfway up the gorge. The only person I spoke to was an old herdsman and during our conversation he mentioned that some relatives of his had been Chris Bonington's porters to Mount Kongur. The herdsmen had taken their oldest and sickest yaks on the trip, hoping that they would die, because although the pay wasn't much, the Chinese government had promised compensation for any yaks that died on the expedition.

The river had cut its gorge through different rock strata, and from shale I entered a conglomerate area with large pebbles embedded in rock. There didn't seem to be any arable land. The sparse dwellings blended into the scenery so well (being made of the same materials) that they were almost invisible. From one bank I spotted a group of beehive-shaped huts. Often I got out of the canoe to reconnoitre along the bank, and if necessary to lift the canoe around an impassable rapid, but I was unprepared for disaster when it struck.

An innocent ledge jettisoned the canoe into a barrage of rocks and a maelstrom current which pushed me back into a trough of churning water at the bottom of the ledge. Water flooded into the canoe. I was petrified and the shock of the icy water pouring over me nearly immobilised me. I tried to paddle free but the paddle blades kept hitting rocks. Then as we came clear, the canoe reared up against a partly submerged rock and to my horror I was overturned. My hands scrabbled at the slippery rocks, anything to get out of the freezing water, but I could get no hold. So I floundered toward the bank, gasping with fright, swimming a rapid in the process but without injury, and got washed up on the shore. My canoe was still in the river, ahead of me, and forgetting my numbness I charged after it. It jammed across a rapid then went through. I ran for all I was worth. Fortunately it stuck again against some rocks and I was able to grab its rope and pull it on to the shore. The paddle arrived in its wake. For a moment I lay coughing up water on the ground beside the canoe, then kicked myself into action again. The cold was intense and I shivered uncontrollably while I emptied the canoe of water and righted its contents. Everything was wet but nothing important was missing.

In some ways I wanted to stop my canoe journey then and

there, but a small voice inside me said that I should paddle on at least until reaching a good place to climb out of the gorge and rejoin the road. Despite my wet clothes and miserable state, my spirits picked up again as I continued downriver. It would be hard to stay depressed in such magnificent landscape. Red rocky mountains towered above the craggy grey gorge. But within a short distance I started shaking with cold and decided to abandon the river. It was late afternoon. After deflating and packing away my canoe I got a lift back to Kashgar in an army truck. As we came down to the lowlands and out between red cliffs I glanced behind and saw some of the peaks I had passed earlier, now receding into the distance.

Before leaving Kashgar and heading back east along the Silk Road, I went to a Kazakh wedding celebration. The invitation was written on a slip of paper in Arabic with a sketch of feasting and musicians. At 6 p.m. I was taken to the house, set inside a courtyard. On a wooden balcony musicians were playing the flute, lute, violin, drum and xylophone, making Russian-style dance music. Three men were dancing in a way that reminded me of the Cossack dances I'd seen on films; they slapped hands, not clapping, and shook their shoulders, spinning and stamping, using small, fast footsteps, with arms outstretched and head held proudly. After half an hour we were beckoned inside the house and sat on the floor with some men in a richly carpeted room. Everyone sat in rows against the tapestried walls. The bridegroom was in the centre of one line of dark capped heads, a tall shy-looking man about twenty-five years old. He told me his name was Kardi Honhoying, and I thanked him for letting me be there, with the few words I could remember of Uighur. A man brought in an ornate metal teapot and bowl and went around the room for each of us to wash our hands. The bowl had a false bottom so that the waste water fell neatly out of sight. Then large dishes of food were brought; soupy vegetables and meat, which everyone dipped into with chopsticks, it was spicy and delicious. We had local flat breads to go with it, and tea.

After this initial course there was more dancing and music. It was all men – the women were sitting in a side room. I went to join them for a while, and to find out who was the bride. The women welcomed me, but they said that the bride was not there, she was at another house where an equal amount of feasting was going on. While we talked someone brought trays laden with *pilau* of rice and mutton. The women laughed at the way I used chopsticks and gave me a wooden spoon.

Outside the door the dancers twirled and stomped. People kept arriving to give presents to the groom. After each part of the feast everyone gave thanks to Allah for what they had received, asking his blessing. At the end of the fourth course everyone stood up, and seizing the bridegroom they surged in a chanting mob out of the house, across the yard and into the dark alley. Still mobbing the groom and calling for blessings they threaded their way through the night, across town to another house, along a dark tunnel. We emerged into a court-yard with multi-level balconies and a high-ceilinged room where one man and a bunch of women sat. They were fat and wore white veils under their skull-caps, though not over their faces. This was the family of the bride, Bu Hlichen, and the man, her father, wore a black kaftan and white turban. Musicians arrived. People sat around chatting and giving more presents to the groom.

Late in the night I left and made my way home along the dark alleys. Some were completely unlit, unnerving when you meet people. Fortunately I knew my way around town by now, and with relief I came to the mosque square, an area faintly lit by street lights and some market stalls still open for food. Kebabs and ice cream by candlelight. The candles have extra thick wicks so they don't blow out in the breeze. Towards the hotel it got dark again and the last half-mile was an uphill trudge, but I managed to hitch a ride on a donkey cart which had nearly run me down.

Before leaving Kashgar I went to the Public Security Office to extend my visa. The normal extension is a month, but I asked for a six-week extension. The police officer regarded me solemnly and said that he couldn't possibly give me six weeks, however he could give me forty-five days. I accepted it meekly.

5　Desert cities

The desert was in flower. In the time between my outward bus journey from Urumchi and my return across the Taklamakan there were now masses of pale yellow lupins. Even in the driest areas the thorny shrubs had tiny yellow trumpet flowers, and others had pussy-willow shaped heads of red and yellow stamens. One evening the bus broke down in the middle of nowhere. The ground was baked mud and quartz pebbles, many white quartzes streaked with yellows, pinks, oranges and blacks.

On the last day we drove into a colossal sand-storm. It started as a yellow cloud on the horizon and quickly expanded to cover the sky. We had to drive extra slowly against the wind. Poplar trees strained to bend over at right angles. Animals huddled with their backs to the wind, and truck loads of straw mats were being blown off their vehicles. It blew for over an hour. But it was probably minuscule in comparison to the sand-storm which buried those three hundred cities in twenty-four hours.

I had a chance to see some of these ruined cities of the Silk Road when I reached Turfan, five hours by bus from Urumchi in the Turfan Depression, which lies about 450 feet below sea level and would soon be an inferno of heat. It is known in that part of the Gobi as the land of fire. The place I had read about was the ruins of Gaochang. I hitched a lift across a desert devoid even of camel-thorn. Gaochang lies several miles from the main road but I didn't mind walking the last bit. It's more exciting to enter a ruined city on foot. This one covers about 250 acres of desert.

The hot sun and gritty air, like a thick sand-fog, intensified the feeling of desolation as I passed through gaps in the mammoth outer wall where the clay has fragmented into rows of stumpy finger-shaped pillars. The corner towers are still discernible, though the main gateway is just an empty space looking on to a desert of grey stones. A dried-up river-bed runs between the city's outer and inner walls; perhaps the place was abandoned when the river stopped running.

The city was built around AD 100 and the dynasty which ruled from here had lasted until AD 600; one of its kings married a princess of the Tang dynasty and Gaochang became capital of Central Asia's most influential province. It was abandoned in the fourteenth century. Many of the buildings have been knocked down since then by peasant farmers who used the earth for growing crops, and frescoes have been pounded up because their pigments were believed to make good fertiliser. Today the state keeps better care of its national monuments.

Dust-devils swirled in the empty streets and were my only companions for a while. I walked along alleyways between a jumble of fallen structures. The air was so thick with dust that despite climbing up to vantage points on walls I couldn't see the whole city. I realised that there are three sets of enclosing walls, those of the outer and inner city and the palace city. But none of the walls has kept out the forces of nature and gradual disintegration. A ghostly place. The only life I could see was some black beetles and spiky ground weed. The best-preserved building is a monastery. Its walls enclose a large domed edifice and a tower with niches that once bore statues. German archaeologists at the beginning of the century discovered a six-foot fresco of a man with a halo, attended by disciples. They realised that it probably portrayed Manes, the third-century Persian mystic and founder of Manichaeism, based on the principles of light and dark. It would be the only picture of Manes ever to be found. Manes himself was killed as a heretic and his followers fled eastward, their influence radiating on down the Silk Road, and still evident in various parts of Xinjiang, where some fine examples of Manichaean art have been found.

The German archaeologists also found a small Nestorian Christian church outside the city walls containing Byzantine-style murals. Nestorius had been exiled from Europe by the Council of Ephesus (AD 432). His disciples also went east along the Silk Road, as missionary-traders, establishing footholds for their religion, which still existed when Marco Polo came this way in the late thirteenth century.

Some tourists turned up in a taxi and offered me a lift to a place of tombs several miles away. They were Hong Kong Chinese, garrulous and raucous, yet full of good humour and obviously enjoying themselves. They spoke Cantonese, not Mandarin, and some English. The seventh-century Hastana tombs are underground, but tomb shafts have been opened up by excavation. We walked down their throats and into vaults with painted walls. In the first vault human faces were drawn in black outlines on a white background, the second vault portrayed richly coloured ducks, geese and cranes. The third held two corpses, a man and a woman, well preserved by the ultra-dry climate. Their skin was like parchment, shrunken and dusty. Below the empty staring eye-sockets were mouths with teeth in good condition, not even stained. Each corpse had a piece of wood in its mouth. The man's mouth was open, as though frozen in the act of calling out. Their legs were bandaged but no other grave clothes survived. The archaeological explorer Sir Aurel Stein had cut the silk robes off some of the bodies when he came here in 1915. It's popular nowadays to label as thieves the various archaeologists who took the treasures of the ruined cities back to their own countries, but at the time they were honoured and both Hedin and Stein received knighthoods for their work (although neither was born British).

The international race for antiquities from Chinese Turkestan included archaeological expeditions from seven countries, among them Russia and Japan. Between them they took a fortune, but at least they preserved their finds somewhere, unlike a local farmer, who dug up huge quantities of ancient manuscripts in 1906 but, being frightened that he could be punished if he kept them, destroyed them all in the river.

My companions had gone, they were outside taking photographs of each other in the desert. The taxi drove us to another site; it was a lovely road, running alongside a range of magnificent red mountains. These are called the Flaming Mountains because when the sun blazes down on the rocks they're reputed to blaze with flame colours and radiate waves of hot air. At the end of the range the dirt road goes along the top of a river canyon, and in its far wall we could see caves hollowed at different levels of the cliff. The taxi-driver said those caves were badly vandalised but he would take us to caves with better frescoes. These were the thousand Buddha caves at Baizeklik, one thousand years old, set in the cliff face above a river bend. The setting was ingenious because the caves could not be seen from the cliff top, and their only entrance was via a steep winding pathway going down the cliff.

Most of the caves were locked by iron gates but a caretaker opened them up for us to go in and admire the frescoes. Several were painted in blue and white, and some were multi-coloured, faces and designs on walls and ceilings, but in a poor state of repair. Other caves had faded frescoes depicting garden scenes, Buddha images, and pedestals and niches where Buddha statues once sat, reclined or stood. The grotto interiors were smoothed with plaster of earth and chopped straw, and the frescoes themselves were painted on to a two-inch thick layer of straw-mud mixture. But nearly all have been vandalised, both by the great race for antiquities when frescoes were hacked out to take abroad, and equally by Moslem fanatics who defaced almost every face and gouged out the eyes. There are ceilings painted with scores of Buddha heads, each one painstakingly vandalised. Other frescoes have been damaged by Russian emigrés who used the caves as hideouts. Tomb-robbers must also account for damage. One of Stein's finds of statues was smashed to pieces by tomb-robbers looking for hidden treasure inside the statues.

Among the Indian, Persian and East Asian physical types portrayed in the statues and frescoes found here there was one man with red hair, blue eyes, and European features. Europeans who penetrated this far included a few captured by the Mongol army (who integrated into the Nogai minority tribe), and some soldiers from the armies of Alexander the Great, sweeping Greek culture as far as these mountains, where some of the soldiers had settled down to live. Graeco-Buddhist art was one of the results.

Another day I hired a donkey-cart and drove ten miles west of Turfan to the once-fabled city of Jiaohe. The donkey didn't want to trot away from his home territory and he kept kicking out backwards. Several of his kicks were cleverly aimed above the cart edge but they missed both me and the taxi-boy. When the donkey settled down he worked well, pulling at a good pace, even on the last part of the drive which goes over the river and up the steep-sided island. Jiaohe stands on a high bluff island in the confluence of two rivers. Its name means Between the Streams. It had been the capital of the Che Shi Qian kingdom from about 200 BC until mid-AD 500 and was destroyed by Genghiz Khan.

The main street used to run north to south. Some of the mud-brick buildings are reasonably intact, including a monastery at the northern end. There are arches and window-holes, narrow passageways and sunken storage rooms with oval ceilings, a strange townscape of smooth dry mud. Walking through gave me a feeling that obliterated all sense of time, yet all the vastness of the ages was contained there. The whole city is only about a hundred yards wide, as wide as the island whose sheer cliffs drop vertically into two canyons and were more effective than city walls.

Our route back to Turfan had roadworks in progress, with many mule- and donkey-drawn carts loading earth and rocks. The animals were encouraged forward with yells of 'Chu-ah'. People were working hard, hurrying and getting on with it; there was none of the idleness that one hears criticised in big-town factory workers. As we trotted into the thriving baked-mud town which is Turfan, I paused to visit the Imim Pagoda, a tall, tapering pagoda whose exterior bricks form geometric patterns. Inside is a spiral staircase leading to the top. It was built by Suleiman the Great as a gesture of thanks to the Qing government for its trust in his family and its permission to preach Islam. The pagoda towers over a mosque which stands on a platform with walls and a gatehouse.

Turfan was a kingdom in the fifteenth century, but unlike Jiaohe, it is a living relic of the past. I enjoyed being there. Its alleys are dusty and narrow, hemmed in between mud-walled courtyards. Brick-making is a chore done along the roadsides, mixing mud with straw and setting it as bricks in wooden frames. Some roads are bordered by water dykes and slender poplar trees. Many courtyard gateways were closed by double wooden gates studded with nails, other gates were open and gave me glimpses into courtyards with mud houses and mud balustrades. The swept clay yards were partly shaded by grape vines. No grapes yet; the vines were in blossom with tiny green flowers that gave off an airy fragrance. Just inside some open gates one household was making big wooden chests and decorating their tops and fronts with thin metal strips in crossed and fan patterns. Both husband and wife were nailing the strips on, first using an awl to punch a hole then fitting a small nail and hammering it home. The hammers were locally made and roughly shaped. Their youngest son brought me a bowl of tea, which I gratefully accepted. Their elder son was assembling the wooden frame of a new chest, without nails; he used wooden pegs dipped in local glue to cement the joints. With jingling bells, a donkey trotted past outside, ridden by a serenely smiling wizened old Uighur, bouncing along on its rump.

In another alley I followed the sound of an odd vibrating twang, which led me to an open-fronted workshop where three young boys were teasing out a mound of raw cotton fluff. Their tools and methods probably haven't changed much since cotton became important here in ancient times. One boy was pulling handfuls of cotton over a board with many sharp pegs separating the wadges. The second boy spread the cotton on to a large table and the eldest youth fluffed up the fibres by twanging a taut wire through them. Taking a long notched pole and thread, the two began binding the cotton into a blanket, waving the pole, catching the thread, criss-crossing the blanket to hold the cotton in place. Finally the whole thing was flattened, using wooden slabs with an ironing motion, and folded to make the innards of bed-quilts, standard bedding in homes and hotels of Xinjiang.

A deaf-mute Uighur girl took me through her house-yard to see a field of cotton being grown, young plants, only an inch tall. Back in her yard she showed me the mulberry trees which provide fodder for silkworms which are commonly reared around here. To obtain the silk, the local people unravel the cocoons on wooden reels, combining the fine silken strands together into silk thread. The Chinese had zealously guarded the secrets of silk production for three thousand years, until the fifth century when two Persian monks discovered the secrets and smuggled some silkworm eggs and mulberry seeds out of China.

Feeling hungry, I took the deaf-mute girl out to supper at the bazaar. We went to a street stall which sold hunks of cooked meats and goats' heads. My new friend chose a slab of mutton for us and, like everyone else there, we ate it with our hands. Perhaps some of our easy friendship was because, not having language, she has developed her ability to communicate without it. Her expressions and gestures carried more meaning than I could have understood in words of any language. The bazaar had an array of barrows laden with dried fruit, sunflower seeds, yellow powders and green vegetables; groups of men with wispy beards were sitting on stools working away on their shoe-repairing machines. Shoes are seldom allowed to die of old age and are continually being re-soled, heeled and stitched. Behind the bazaar is the donkey and cart parking-lot, where I found myself a lift back to the hotel.

Without any doubt the evenings and the early mornings are the best times of day in Turfan, while midday is akin to being in a dusty furnace. Yet this was the safest time of day for me to practise donkey-cart driving, when not many others were in the alleys. I had persuaded an old man to give me a few driving lessons, because I wanted to be more proficient at it and Turfan seemed a good place to learn in. The tight alley corners, twisting lanes, and other traffic give a fair challenge. I sat back and studied the way the old man harnessed his donkey; one sound meant 'Come along', another 'Go backwards', or 'Your hoof is caught in the harness, stand still'. To my ear the commands sounded rather identical, but the donkey knew the difference. The harness was home-made, a collar stuffed with straw and reinforced with a rubber strip off an old truck tyre. Its two ends were bound with leather thongs and decorated with coloured pompoms. The old man, Ahmet, was a cobbler but he looked more like a philosopher, which to some extent he was. He seemed to have absorbed the bumps and jolts of life in the same way as his thin body sat on the cart, flexible and well-balanced, with his face relaxed into a total lack of expression.

Ahmet's warning grunt came too late and the cart's wheels slid into a set of ruts. 'When you're stuck in a rut it's hard to get free,' he pointed out. 'You must learn to recognise the pitfalls in advance.' The ruts flattened out into dust and I took a turning out of the town in the direction of the nearby lake at Aydingkol. This lake, at about 500 feet below sea level, is the lowest point in China and the second lowest in the world. Out in the desert the cart rattled and thumped over the bumps. Since we were keeping up a smart trot, the driving took all my concentration and there were some hairy moments. So I slowed the donkey's pace and we ambled along, creaking gently. In the irrigated village oases, horse-drawn ploughs were being used to till the earth, harrowing one furrow at a time. A man on horseback came by herding twenty goats along with a rope whip, and a passing vendor sold me a length of sugarcane that was superbly juicy and sweet.

Turfan's heat makes it especially suitable for grapevines; the grapes are turned into raisins and sultanas, and the ones I'd eaten were so good they deserve their reputation. The valley where they grow best is an eight-mile stretch of lush green vines. In contrast to the town's flowering grapevines these had already begun forming fruit, and their flowers lay scattered on the ground.

For water, Turfan's agriculture relies on the *karez* system. This ingenious network of underground channels and wells was invented by the Persians 2,000 years ago. The *karez* run underground for many miles and emerge as open irrigation channels where required. I watched a man moving the stone slabs that blocked the junction of five channels, diverting the water to different areas. Ducks quacked as their dry pond began to fill, and children arrived with donkeys harnessed to empty water barrels. In three hours the slabs would be moved again and the water re-directed. With this system, Turfan grows everything necessary for life in abundance.

Ahmet's donkey had at her side her latest youngster, who was also getting some training. There's no need for man to break-in a donkey, it learns from infancy to run beside its mother, and to do what she does on the appropriate command. The commands become instinctive when learnt that early. Perhaps our troubles with disobedient donkeys in England are because we don't catch them young enough. The penalties for disobedience can be heavy and I'd noticed some cruelty from taxi-boys angrily hitting their donkeys' raw backbones with rocks. Uighur people are not good with animals; they are too impatient, their strength is in agriculture. The Mongols and Kazakhs are said to be the best at handling animals. Ahmet is Uighur, but has patience. He needed it to teach me to drive; he stayed calm even when I miscalculated a bridge and ended up with one wheel in a ditch. Perhaps I'll never make an ace charioteer.

On my last evening in Turfan I went to a display of song and dance by local Uighur girls. The opening dance was set to the rousing music of eight men playing traditional Uighur violins and rattles, an accordion, drums, and a snake-charmer type of bugle. Four girls whose hair was braided into plaits down as far as their hips, wore puce gowns and black embroidered jackets, and danced in restrained and stately fashion, their arms swaying and wrists twisting in flowing angular movements, while a solo female singer sang a high almost operatic song. Two comic songs followed, with men making amorous advances and women playing coy. The audience (many of whom were Uighur) laughed uproariously at the song's words, which were undoubtedly bawdy. The musical solos had the same nasal quality as a neighing horse. The liveliest dance was that of a young girl accompanied by a snake-skin drum, she writhed and flexed every limb, her body bending over backward to touch the ground then rising and whirling away in circles. The grape-harvesting dance was another local favourite. The girls gracefully plucking grapes from the air, tasting them, twirling away because they were so bitter, and finding more imaginary bunches. I was impressed with the way they danced right down to their finger tips. Marco Polo had observed that the people of Hami (an oasis nearby) 'are addicted to pleasure, and attend to little else than playing upon instruments, singing, dancing . . . every kind of amusement'. He added that when strangers come to stay, the husband orders his wives and daughters, who are 'handsome and sensual women', to gratify every wish of their guests. When adultery became illegal, this region was exempted because their hospitality was of such long tradition.

6   Heaven Lake and solitude

My plan was to see a little more of China's northern Gobi, so I left most of my luggage in Urumchi and took my camping gear and my canoe on the bus to Tianchi to visit a famous beauty spot, known as Heaven Lake. It's a popular day-trip for tourists but I hoped to trek a bit further afield. When the bus stopped at the tourist lodge by the lake the passengers trooped off, chattering noisily. I was among the first off the bus and was soon striding away carrying my backpack and heading along a path towards the far end of the lake.

To my surprise the lake was frozen over. Sun glistened on the ice and on the very snowy mountains at its far end. It was a breath-taking scene. My speed didn't slacken until I came to the end of the well-made path and started treading a rougher trail. The track along the lakeshore followed a jumble of rocky headlands divided by grassy coves and another trail higher up ran through pine woods. From the higher one I could see more clearly over the long, narrow lake. In the middle of the ice there was a well defined line from north to south along the length; a footpath used by local people as a winter short-cut. In mid-winter it's probably safer than scrambling over the slippery rocks, and now in spring I could see some cracks beginning to form. I chucked a rock at the ice near the lakeside but it didn't break.

At the head of the lake was a pile of glacial moraine; the present-day glaciers have retreated further up the mountains and the river which flows from them enters the lake underneath the moraine. I decided to follow the river up to where it melts out of the glacier and to canoe what I could of it on the way down. It took me a day to walk up, with frequent stops to gasp for breath in this thin air, and I spent the night in an empty log-cabin. From the pine forest I emerged above the tree line into alpine grasslands and continued upwards through a snowy landscape. There were no footprints in the snow, only the tracks of an antelope. One more gulley crossing, slithering on the loose, icy scree, brought me on to the glacier. I picked my way cautiously down its nose to where the trickle of water began, though I could hear it long before it was visible as it ran hidden beneath a cover of ice and snow. The stream's first steep drop was fronted by a cascade of icicles. It made me laugh at myself for being so absurd as to think that one could canoe out of a glacier. About half a mile further it was a running stream and where this joined another small stream it became deep enough for my canoe. I was impatient to be afloat, although I suddenly dreaded the thought of capsizing in that cold water.

In my hurry to pump up the canoe I overworked the foot pump and it split along one seam, but a makeshift patch of plumber's tape mended it well on a temporary level. By the time the canoe was ready to put in the stream I felt exhausted. Every task took more energy because of the thin air. I guessed the glacier's foot to be at about 14,500 feet. I wondered why the altitude hadn't affected me so much around Mount Kongur and Lake Karakol. Perhaps because I had ridden up by truck, and I was always descending, and as you descend, breathing gets easier. This time I'd come from below sea level, and climbed a fair height on foot, carrying my rucksack. It had been demanding. Fortunately I don't suffer from altitude sickness.

Before settling myself inside the canoe I took a last look at the stretch of stream ahead, then set off. Here in its headwaters it was only a small brook, studded with boulders, and often there was barely room for my canoe to pass between. We scraped against many boulders but it didn't worry me, the rocks were smooth and I felt sure the canoe could take a fair bit of punishment, and I was in no danger because the water's speed was minimal. Shoving my paddle into the rocky bed I poled us through some narrow gaps, and frequently put down the paddle to push away the rocks by hand. Where the stream went beneath patches of snow and ice I had to get out and portage, and also where waterfalls made paddling impossible. Portage is simple because I can carry the canoe under my arm. At some steep little chutes I took the precaution of leaving my camping gear on the bank, before canoeing the chutes, then came back for it on foot. The idea of a wet sleeping bag didn't appeal to me. Despite the sunshine the air was very cold. Now that we were again lower than the tree line there was deep snow lying in drifts against the pines. When I looked at my watch I saw with surprise that it showed 6 p.m. – no wonder I was tired and hungry – and I looked out for the log-cabin where I had spent the previous night. From my seat on its doorsill I could see the summits glowing in the last rays of sun. This is the Tien Shan range. The highest mountain is Bogda Ola (Mountain of

God) at about 20,000 feet (6,000m). I couldn't tell which peak it was, there were several giants nearby and others beyond them.

Sunset was at 8 p.m. but darkness didn't come until after ten. However, the intense cold drove me into my sleeping bag long before dark. I sat up writing my diary, stoking my fire and sipping coffee. Occasional explosive bangs from the fire spat red embers on to my covers and dry grass bed; the bangs gave me a fright every time and the sparks made me twist round extinguishing them. Not so peaceful.

It was snowing when I woke at dawn. When it stopped I went for a walk. My body felt cramped and cold so I went up the mountains behind the hut, though I had to pause every thirty paces to gasp for breath. As the sun gradually melted the snow I saw celandines, anemones, and a lot of young wild rhubarb. All the colours, including the blue sky, seemed to be made more vivid by the rarefied air. How wonderful it was to be in a landscape where there were not any people, and I saw none for the whole of that day. It made me realise how crowded I'd felt in the past week, always among people. With a population of a billion, it must be rare in China for anyone to find himself alone for long stretches; the Chinese don't like to be alone, and visitors seldom get the chance. Even in the Pamirs I'd seen occasional people. Up here in summer there would be nomadic Kazakh herdsmen searching among the top slopes for pasture. The cabin where I had stayed was their overnight shelter. But now the mountains were empty. The feeling of having the whole landscape to myself brings a special pleasure which is exclusive and deep; it can have the intensity of love. Solitude gives time for thought, and open spaces have the right proportions, with changing perspectives and an echoing silence.

The next section of river was nearly impossible because its course dropped steeply down a bed of boulders. I slid over the slippery rocks and splashed into the pools below mushroom-shaped cascades. As the canoe approached one chute I realised it was one that I hadn't meant to try, with a vertical drop of ten feet, but I hadn't been able to see this until the canoe came to its rim. Back-paddling furiously I stopped the canoe going forward, but couldn't manage to back up further or change course. Without really thinking, I jumped out of the canoe into the rocky shallows, pulling the canoe to safety behind me. A half-soaking was the technique that I developed over the rest of that day, hopping out whenever something looked too terrifying.

When I had first arrived at the lake it had been frozen over fairly solidly, but in the intervening time that I'd spent in the mountains it had begun to thaw. There were cracks opening up right across it, dividing the ice sheet like crazy paving. There was already a ten-foot wide clear channel between the ice and the shore, so I paddled along it. The rocky shore shelved deeply, and the water was coloured turquoise-blue by glacial sediments, and despite the splashing of my paddle I could hear the tinkling and creaking of melting ice. It had a pure and brittle quality.

That night I camped in a cove by the lakeshore, and managed to dry my clothes over a fire. By building the fire against some sheltered boulders I heated up one boulder enough to keep me warm, and it was a mild night. By morning the ice had thawed further and the cracks had widened into paths. Eagerly I set out paddling across the lake. It was a glorious morning, crisp with the ever-present sound of ice breaking up, and made dazzlingly bright by the sun on the ice. In two of the inlets on the far shore I could see yurts, though without any smoke coming from their roofs as a sign of occupation. My canoe was quite far out across the lake when a breeze from the north began to shift the broken ice-plates down the lake. They moved slowly, almost imperceptibly and, being a long narrow lake, they began to scrunch together at the southern end where I was paddling. When plates collided they rubbed against each other until one of them was forced to submerge and the other was thrust up on to it. I wondered what I'd do if my path closed, presumably we would capsize, and feeling the splintered sharpness of the ice edges made me suspect that the canoe would be punctured in many places.

I began to paddle a little faster toward a wider path. It was like paddling through mobile crazy paving. The route I'd hoped to take became closed, and one to the side opened up, yet when I was in it it began to narrow. With some urgency I back-paddled; there was no room to turn around, and the paddle blades struck the ice unless I put them close beside the canoe. Back-paddling and glancing over my shoulder I realised with dismay that I was too late, the crack was closing, and although it moved infinitely slowly I would not get there in time. When it came to the crunch I stuck my paddle against the smaller ice-plate and pushed it, a long steady push. The crack was no longer narrowing; it didn't look as though my pushing was doing any good yet it was obviously having an effect.

Once free of that situation I headed for the closest point of land, and found that as we got nearer the shore the ice was thinner and easier to push aside. The danger was over. To record the experience I paused to take a couple of photographs with the camera which I'd attached to the canoe's nose. It isn't difficult to trigger the self-timer on flat water, but a sudden frantic bleeping announced that the film had ended. Its instructions said rewind immediately. I nearly panicked with the shock of that noise, but when I tried to reach the camera I couldn't manage it, and as I crept forward the canoe started to wobble. A new air leak had made one side-tube too soft for stability, I couldn't even kneel up and grab the camera. Its bleeping was raucous, impossible to ignore; it would drive me mad before I could reach the shore and I made one more lunge forward to grasp it. My hand hit it and I grabbed hold, but it was too well-taped into place and because it didn't come off my balance was all wrong. With an icy feeling of surprise I overbalanced sideways into the lake. I came to the surface gasping with cold, flung my arms and shoulders over the canoe, and swam using it as giant water-wings. My feet were numb but my legs were kicking in determination to reach the shore. The infernal camera was still bleeping.

Scrambling on to the shore I pulled the canoe up behind me, and rushed along to the cove where I had spent the night, thinking only of reviving the fire and changing into the dry clothes I'd left there in my backpack. But before I changed I took the camera and tore at its taped wrapping, trying to find the rewind button and wishing that I'd had the forethought to read the instructions. Finally my efforts succeeded, the spool rewound and the bleeper went silent. I hoped the film would be worthwhile. 'If I don't die of pneumonia first,' I muttered as I stripped out of my wet things and looked for my towel. For warming exercise I rambled around the lakeshore for several hours and in the evening I felt ready enough to trade my precious solitude for a night in the tourist lodge. In the event I was their only guest. They installed me in a wooden bungalow which had a wood stove in the bedroom. It was marvellous to dry out my soaked clothes and even though there was no running water or hot bath, I managed a tepid strip-wash.

Next morning I walked to the northern end of the lake, looking for its river outlet. As I passed near a circular yurt a large dog came bounding over snarling. I picked up a stone. The dog paused but kept on snarling and when he realised that I hadn't thrown the stone he came closer in a frenzy of barking yellow teeth. So I threw it and grabbed for more, and began calling the yurt's occupants to help me. A young woman pulled back the door curtain and coming hastily outside she called and cursed the dog, which loped off sulkily. I went over to say good morning. She looked to be about my age, and living so near the lodge she was used to seeing foreigners. She invited me into the yurt for a cup of tea, which was a welcome idea. On the old pot-bellied stove in the centre, a kettle was already boiling. The girl, who said her name was Bentilash, poured tea into two dishes and added some sour goat's milk which tasted salty and warming. We sat on floormats of wool laid on swept earth. Two toddlers lay on sheepskins covered by blankets and a baby slept in a wooden cradle. Bentilash said that only one child was hers, the other two belonged to women who had gone off into the hills for the day. They were all Kazakh people. Kazakhs were once part of the Mongol Golden Horde, until they became an independent nomadic group in the sixteenth century. Their territory was taken away by Russia in the nineteenth century and nowadays about a million Kazakhs live in China while about seven million live in Russia.

Outside the yurt I could hear the wind buffeting the felt, but inside was a haven of warmth. There was no question of the yurt being blown down because it was secured by ropes and had a round wooden trellis framework inside. From this hung things of daily use; shoulder bags, woven straps and felt hats; around the walls were pots and pans, water jars of carved wood and brooms of twigs; there were some shelves and a tea chest (similar to those I'd seen being made in Turfan) and on the walls hung decorative tapestries in red, black and yellow floral designs.

When the children woke up, Bentilash put jackets on them before she let them go outside and on their return she poured milky tea into bowls and spread some dry chunks of bread on a wooden board. We dipped them in our tea. According to Bentilash most of the other Kazakh people were still down in the lowlands with their herds, though they would soon be migrating up into their summer grasslands.

The trail which the animals follow came from down in the valley behind Bentilash's yurt and when I left I followed this. It zigzagged downhill not far from the stream out of Heaven Lake, which fell in a series of mossy waterfalls before flowing into a *karez* system. That would have been a fright by canoe, falling down chutes into narrow irrigation canals which probably vanish underground for miles. Fortunately I had by this time reverted to being a backpacker. Part of the pleasure of the canoe is that it takes only fifteen minutes to inflate or pack away. With its water usurped by the karez, and not being flood season, the river-bed continued onward as a dry pebble course.

A horse came galloping along the bank, ridden by a young man in a hurry. The Kazakhs are renowned horsemen and famous for the horses they breed. They call their horses their 'wings' and often value them above their wives. This horse was wild-eyed and foaming with sweat; it raced past and was gone. Further down along the river-bank I came to where a group of Kazakh people, in the process of migration, were coming to make their summer camp. The earliest arrivals had started unpacking their laden oxen but many were still on the move, riding on horseback and driving their herds of horses, sheep and goats ahead of them. Some drove cattle that were laden with boxes and bundles, rolls of felt, trunks strapped in A-shapes over their backs, long bundles of poles and an assortment of buckets. The widest load was on a bullock that carried a six-foot bed. One man was riding his horse and carrying five large bundles, with other packages strapped to the saddle. It was a lovely image of moving house. To keep out of harm's way, young children sometimes rode with their father, and in the general mill of action I saw several women on horseback, controlling their difficult steeds without apparent effort.

Splitting into family groups, they laid claim to the hillocks and raised banks of the dry river, and began to unpack. At each chosen plot the quantity of possessions grew into large heaps, in which round-faced children played tumbling games until ordered to stop by their elders. Another popular but dis-approved of game was playing horse-riding on the saddles which sat on the ground. Their tall pommels, high backs and cloth or sheepskin padding made them a comfortable ride. Some were very ordinary and some were treasures with inlaid silver decoration.

It was nearly midday and I was in no hurry so I joined a friendly group and kept their children amused while they got on with erecting the yurt. Actually the children didn't need entertainment, they just sat and stared at me through their slanting almond-shaped eyes for almost an hour. Spreading out the sections of criss-crossed red willow poles, the bigger children and six adults pulled them out until long enough to be the yurt's circular wall. To support the ceiling some eight-foot

willow wands were slotted at an angle into a wide open circle
at the top (the smoke hole). When I asked one of the men why
the poles are dyed red he replied that the dye protects the
wood. We talked in a smattering of Chinese plus gestures. The
walls are made of felt from sheep-wool. This yurt would also
have an inner wall of straw matting. It would be a good form
of insulation. I suppose that tapestries and wall-carpets are
basically for insulation too.

When the children became restless they found some wooden
ox-saddles to play with, permissible toys, so I left my rucksack
beside the heaps of family possessions and went for a stroll to
see what else was happening. An elderly man in a ragged black
fur-lined coat and boots had set himself up as the repairer of
badly damaged yurt frames. He had stockpiles of red canes set
aside to sell to families who had not yet arrived. When complete
the camp would have about sixty families. He worked with a
speed born of years of practice. Looping a leather thong around
each pole-joint, he pulled the knots neatly tight before cutting
them off with a hunting knife he kept between his teeth when
not in use.

Once one family had accepted me, several others invited me
into their yurts for tea. Walking through the camp you can tell
who is at home because their door curtains are rolled up or tied
aside. I met two girls with copper-coloured hair. For a moment
I thought it was the sun playing tricks but when they beckoned
me over I realised that the colour was real. The girls told me it
wasn't that rare, a few others in different communes also
have that colouring. But it was curious because I'd grown so
accustomed to only seeing black-haired Chinese that I thought
of them almost as freaks. It didn't look like a pigment deficiency,
more likely a throwback to some previous generation of ances-
tors.

We drank tea, the saltiness and the watery globs of milk
tasted good. I showed them my photographs; it was a shame I
didn't have a picture of a Western red-head. Like most Kazakh
women, their faces had a full and womanly quality, accentuated
by their broad foreheads and high cheekbones. Home was a
spacious round yurt with embroidered cushions and floor rugs,
some so old they were only held together by their embroidery.
There was something in yurt life which appealed strongly to
me. Perhaps it was the warm hospitality of the old metal stoves
with a kettle keeping hot on the hearth to replenish your tea
whenever it is finished, or the attraction of a life which flows

with the seasons. Perhaps the nomads' success in living their insecure existence comes from not believing in or clutching at the illusion of stability. Their yurt homes show what we house-dwellers may have forgotten, that security is a state of mind.

More people, pack oxen and herds kept arriving but the camp didn't get crowded, they just spread out further across the open space. People hurried to and fro, horses whinnied and snorted. It being springtime, many animals had produced their young; baby goats played jumping, butting games with each other, and there were kittens, calves and foals. When the men decided to begin the making of *kumis*, their national drink of fermented mare's milk, they had to start by wrestling the foals away from the mares. One man got pulled to the ground, but finally brought the foal down by getting hold of its feet, and joined in our laughter when the foal fell over on top of him.

On my last day with the Kazakhs I was taken to watch a game of buzkashi, a sort of polo match with a beheaded goat's body for a ball. My escort soon left me to join in the fray. Buzkashi is a popular sport among the Kazakhs since it involves skilful horseriding and dashes of speed as the players hurtle from one end of the 'field' to tackle whoever has possession of the carcass. The scrum is a free-for-all wrestling match. Women take part as well as men and are equally aggressive. I watched as one seized the carcass with one hand and galloped clinging to the side of her horse, dodging all attempts to stop her. There were no field markers and horses sometimes ran into the crowd, but since most of them were on horseback it didn't matter. I stood with a group near a yurt for protection. The goal was a patch of ground where the riders tried to drop the 'ball', but it was twenty minutes before anyone managed to score. That signalled the end of the game and it was followed almost immediately by a race of women chasing men, again all on horseback. When caught, they hit the men with sticks or their hands. Some men near me explained that the women were capturing their lovers. Afterwards they invited me into the yurt for a meal of boiled mutton with *hurt*, a leathery cheese and *balsac*, a sour-milk bread deep-fried in oil.

I would have liked to spend several months among these people, not just a few days, but it would not have been allowed and I was wasting my time thinking about it. There's no point in longing for what one can't have, especially when we have so much, it's better to get on with what life is offering.

7 Into the Black Gobi

I had now spent five weeks in Xinjiang, out of the four months which were all I would be allowed in China. It was time to move on. I wanted to visit Dunhwang next, the city in Gansu province where the north and south arms of the Silk Road meet. At Dunhwang roads converge from Lhasa, Mongolia, India and Siberia. To get there meant catching a train for the first part of the journey. People advised me that a hard train seat is not a good way to travel if the journey includes nights, though the hard six-berth sleepers are all right, and they recommended paying in local money to get the local price, not the inflated ones for those who pay in tourist money. Tourists in China have plenty of horror stories about the frustrations of queueing for train tickets and the hazards of long-distance journeys, and though I was to suffer my share at the end of my trip, I was lucky in Urumchi.

My companions in the six-berth sleeping compartment were a family of White Russians from Urumchi, three generations of them; the old father, an adult daughter, her husband and two teenage children. When we got talking the lady told me that they had emigrated from Siberia to China when she was seven years old. Now they were on their way to Beijing and flying to Western Australia to visit her married sister for a month. They must be a family of substance. Most of the White Russians in China lost their wealth in the exodus, and their lives no longer include the comforts of former years; they are sensitive to their degradation but accept it without complaint. This family had escaped poverty. Anatoly, the grandfather, seemed a shrewd and kindly man. He showed me their passports, new and crisp, issued specially for the holiday. Passports cannot be easy to obtain; they have to be authorised by the Party headquarters.

The lady pounced on my dictionary and began copying down some English words (she couldn't yet speak any English). We all shared our picnic supper and some people from other seats also wanted me to try a piece of their food. It was a warm, amicable atmosphere. During the journey people wander through the train's carriages selling tired-looking apples, packets of biscuits, eggs and sweets. There is also a dining car which serves a variety of Chinese meals for one to two yuan (under 65p). All carriages are supplied with a tank of boiling water for people to make tea. Everyone brings his own hand-towel, which is hung from a rail above the open windows. The carriage attendants have strict notions on exactly how the towels should be hung. When they see one which isn't correctly folded, they tell the owner to re-hang it properly. Corridor traffic also includes regular forays of people with mops and buckets of water to clean the floors. With everybody spitting and dropping food, the floors get in a nasty state quite quickly. Sometimes when the train stops at oasis stations, men stroll along washing the windows from outside.

For an express our speed wasn't impressive; we trundled along at about thirty miles an hour. The long twilight over the desert faded into darkness. With the reserve that characterises White Russian emigrés the family transformed our compart-ment into a neat enclave, where only a few people stopped to say hello. One of them was an Australian who had visited several places which I wanted to see later. We swapped some maps and up-to-date information from the grapevine: who had tried to travel where and failed or succeeded because of what reason. The latest story was about Peter, the young Dutchman I'd gone to the Pamirs with. The story was being called 'the Firecracker Confession'. It happened when Peter caught this train eastward and put his backpack on the rack. Unfortunately during the night his water bottle leaked. More unfortunately, it was above the guard's head. The guard woke Peter and he tried to get the flask out, but when he untied the bag a whole load of firecrackers fell out. It is illegal to carry explosives on trains. So Peter had to write an official confession. The con-fession of one's misdeeds is considered important by the Party, who like people to see the error of their ways and to repent. Basically they don't accept that people are bad, they are just in temporary need of social instruction, and should be brought to see their mistake. You don't lose face, you change face. Confession has long been an integral part of their legal pro-cedure, and no court-case is complete without one. As a whole, the manners and integrity of the Chinese nation seem remark-able, and as I settled down for the night on the train I felt secure in the feeling that no one would try to steal anything.

Dunhwang is sixty miles from the railway. I had to get there from a one-bus-a-day halt called Liuyuan and of course I missed the bus. So I started to hitch. It was noon and for two hours the only vehicle that passed me was an ice-lolly seller on a bicycle. The lollies were pink or green and refreshing in the hot wind and blistering sun. As I left the depressing little town behind me, I entered a region of Black Gobi. This is virtually the centre point of Asia. To both sides black desert stretches in small conical hills. I wondered if Hell looked like this and sat down to take stock. The wind blew hard and hot and before long a black sand dune had started to build against my lee side. But I was thinking about my grandmother.

My grandmother, Doris Beddow, was one of my reasons for being in China. She had been an unconventional lady and had lived in China for thirty years. My mother was born in Hankow and brought up in Peking, or Beijing as it is now called. Doris had been a special correspondent for the *News Chronicle* and the *Daily News* in the time of the warlords and this enabled her to do quite a bit of travelling. What made me think of her now was an old family snapshot of her sitting in much the same posture as I was in a dust-storm, unconcerned while the dust whirled her hair on end. The photograph in the album was captioned 'D.B. in Hell'. I was looking forward to tracking down some of my family threads when I got to Beijing.

It wasn't until 4 p.m. that a truck came along and stopped, it was an old Romanian truck with a Han driver who said he was going to Dunhwang and would give me a lift. The road wasn't good, or perhaps the truck didn't have springs; the jolting was atrocious and it made me wonder if truck-drivers' teeth fall out more often than other people's teeth. The black desert slowly grew sandier and streaked with browns, and after three hours we saw a herd of camels being driven by men riding camels. The truck driver seemed surprised when I told him that my country has no camels except in zoos.

Approaching Dunhwang there is a sudden transition from desert to oasis, scorched yellow to lush green, almost with a mark like the sea around an island. Before entering the modern town, the truck drove through the remains of a massive city wall and past some huge fragments of buildings with fortified outer walls. This was the site of old Shachow, already a ruin when Marco Polo came this way 750 years ago.

If you are going to explore desert you need a camel. I managed to rent a large old animal to make an excursion to a crescent moon lake. My saddle was a thick, straw-padded mat with two lateral poles and a quilt thrown over it all, and the bridle was simply a nose-peg and rope. The camel kept growling, graunching and trying to stand up during saddling. So I learnt the command 'Zuo' for sit down and sit still. Finally I climbed aboard. When he stood up, my head was about ten feet above ground. The camel's owner accompanied me on another camel to lead the way. Shortly after we had set off my camel got bolshie; he stopped and wouldn't go forward, and when I ordered him to walk he dashed sideways into a thicket of small trees. Unfortunately his nose-peg and rope became hooked on a branch. He panicked and fought to get free, hurting his nose, and as soon as I'd freed him he tried to charge through some trees. I was nearly knocked to the ground but clung on grimly, and when we'd extricated ourselves from the thicket he calmed down.

It wasn't far to the lake and for the rest of the journey he behaved well, swinging his feet across the shallow hills toward a series of large sand dunes and sand mountains where the lake lies. What seems curious to me is that the lake exists at all, since sand dunes are known to move under the force of wind. The lake should have been obliterated by dunes, yet somehow the wind patterns must protect it. According to old records, the lake has been here since before the early Han era, and was ever esteemed for its beauty. The camel-driver told me that on the sixth day of the sixth lunar month, Chinese people still come here to collect a specially medicinal mugwort, and to sit buried in the sand as therapy for aches and pains.

As we came over a slight incline I caught sight of the lake and realised that it had after all shrunk – it is now only a pond; like everything, its source is drying up. My camel stopped to drink and I dismounted to wash my face. It was a shame that broken bottles and empty beer cans littered the ground and floated on the water. In view of the size of the 300-feet high sand mountains beyond the lake and the camel driver's reluctance to take his beasts climbing in them, I decided to go off on foot for the remainder of the day. The camels could go home and I would rejoin them another day. On foot it was heavy going in soft sand as I struggled to climb the first mountain. With each footstep the sand slid downhill beneath me. On reaching the ridge I lay down with my elbows hooked over it, gulped some water from my flask, and gazed out over an ocean of huge dunes, motionless like petrified waves. Between them were valleys and basins of firm rippled sand, and ridges throwing sharply defined shadows. The Gobi is reputed to be full of *kwei*, Yin demons connected with death and darkness. Old travellers' diaries record the illusion of human voices at night in the desert. There are also *shen*, spirits of minor deities who avenge wrongdoing, while *mo* are inhuman demons, wholly evil.

For three hours I kept walking and reached a high choppy plateau. Some of the Gobi's sand dunes are musical underfoot. The big dune opposite the lake is famous for having a noise like thunder, though it is only audible on certain days. Other dunes produce similar drum-roll noises, and some make music without human intervention, being played only by the wind. The phenomenon is not of course limited to the Gobi but there is no clear explanation why usually only one dune will sing while the rest of an area is permanently silent.

At sunset I sat on a ridge overlooking the crescent-shaped lake, and as the sun vanished from sight, a new silver crescent moon rose to echo the shape of the lake. It was a magical, surreal place. About twelve miles east of the crescent lake lie the Magao Caves, which date from the fourth century and shelter the oldest surviving frescoes still in China. Next morning I teamed up with Ellen, a young New Zealand nurse who shared my hotel dormitory, and we caught a public bus to see them. There are about 400 caves, set on different levels of the sandstone cliff face. Where it has crumbled away it reveals their anterooms and interiors. Some are painted with frescoes or hold statues, and they are interconnected by steps and paths. In one cave sat a 100-foot tall statue of Buddha with its base at ground level and its head near the top of the cliff. People still come here to light joss sticks to him. A second big cave has a giant dead Buddha (incarnation of Jakamuni) and on the walls are painted some stunning scenes of mourning, with people of many races showing their grief. Their faces are distorted with sorrow, and they press sword- and knife-points to their chests. Some men are cutting off their ears and noses.

The murals in other caves portray men riding on flying clouds rather like aeroplanes blazing through the sky, or hovering quietly. One cloud has a house on it, and I saw many flying *devis*, mostly in human shape, though a few with chicken legs and wings, flying with streamers of colour trailing out behind them. A red *devi* with gold outlines glittered in my torch's beam. Some frescoes depict scenes from the life of Buddha, or pictorial lists of his incarnations. In many cave entrances the door guardians, painted or moulded, keep vigil against devil spirits, often standing on the snarling pug-faced demons they've caught. Various frescoes give insight into the people's lives, with scenes of men hunting wild animals, battles between armies, soldiers on horseback wearing medieval-type armour, looking like knights at a jousting tournament; peasants tending silkworms and labouring in irrigated fields; and murals of paradise with musicians, artists, scholars and pilgrims flocking to Magao, where many stayed to dedicate their lives to the glory of Buddha.

The dynasties that created this mass of artwork spanned a thousand years. The earliest caves are from the Wei period of AD 380–550, showing an Indian influence from the cradle of Buddhism, with exaggeratedly large men's heads, more detailed than the body, and a propensity for mythical animals. In general their paintings illustrate religious themes, texts and legends. The Sui dynasty which followed was characterised by a Chinese influence, softer lines and more human expressions. Their colours and design are rich and ornate, which is carried to its full extent in the Tang dynasty of AD 600. The Tang produced the most magnificent art, using perspective and technical skill; elaborate yet sensual and with Buddha faces radiating godliness and humility. Some Tang artists specialised in a type of landscape painting known as Shan-shui (Mountain and Water) which illustrates the relationship between man and his environment. A painting can be a philosophical exercise.

Other lesser dynasties made their marks; the Yuan era in AD 1300 has Mongolian influence and a mural technique of flowing movement. They painted the best of the flying *devis*. Various artists used a predominance of red, others preferred indigo blue or a vibrant turquoise. Some painted in outline, some in line-shading or block colour. There was much black which in fact is oxidised red ochre. Every spare inch of wall space not covered by other fresco subjects is painted with Buddha faces, not much bigger than postage stamps, and continuing over whole ceilings like a long-distance letter. The damage done by Moslem fanatics and Western archaeologists did not seem extensive, though some masterpieces here too have been painstakingly defaced. Fortunately the caves have long been protected by preservation orders.

When visited by those intrepid missionary ladies, Mildred Cable and Francesca French, the caves were in the hands of a Taoist priest and self-appointed guardian. He had used the stream to irrigate the land for trees and crops to feed himself and his helpers, and had made begging pilgrimages to raise the money for maintenance of the temples. He also raised money

Mutton for supper in Kashgar.

Work and relaxation in a corner of Kashgar market.

Outside the post office sat the professional letter-writer,
his customers, both westernised and veiled.

The herbalist's at the crossroads of Asia.

Putting the inflatable canoe through its paces
in the river below Mount Kongur.

Kazakh summer migration: the willow frame of a yurt over which the felt is wrapped.

The man who supplied replacement frames.

Tibetan nomad milking her yak.

Sand dunes beyond Dunhwang. At night the Gobi is
full of demons.

A flying *devi* in the Magao Caves.

The fort at the end of the Great Wall, with the snowy peaks of
Qilian Shan on the horizon.

On horseback in the Pamir foothills, by camel
on the border of Inner Mongolia.

Inflatable skin rafts on the Yellow River at Mud Ho.

Giant waterwheels on the Yellow River.

A Tibetan pilgrim at Taer'si lamasery.

Rehearsing for a theatrical performance telling Taer'si's history.

Novice monks are questioned on the scriptures in the main courtyard.

Strange billows of white smoke emerge from the Sichuan mountains,
an area said to be used for missile testing.

The distinctive scenery of Yunnan province.

The stone forest at Shilin.

Above, the surprising headdresses near Shilin;

Top, young girls at the market;

Above, the summit monastery on the sacred mountain,
Ju Jie Shan. Once there had been 350 on the mountain.

Top, old ladies in Binchuan market.

A Bai market.

Yangtse rapids.

Shall we waltz?

Women, at a Bai memorial ceremony on
the way to Dali.

Rafting with style and economy.

Down river from Guilin.

for upkeep by selling some of the 9000 manuscripts which he had discovered in some blocked-up caves. When Aurel Stein came here in 1907 he met the guardian and bought twenty-five cases of scrolls and manuscripts, which he sent back to the British Museum. Some scrolls were written in the most ancient languages of Central Asia. A block-printed roll dating from AD 868 was recognised as being the world's earliest example of a printed book. There was also a set-phrase letter of apology to one's host from guests who had drunk too much and behaved badly (a thousand years ago). In addition, there were some wooden tablets whose clay seals bore pictures of the Greek divinities Eros and Pallas Athene, complete with aegis and thunderbolt. Among the remaining history texts and painted stele records not removed by Aurel Stein is a famous one foretelling the coming of Christianity. The Chinese like to say that Stein was the worst of the pillaging archaeologists who stripped China of so much of her heritage at the beginning of this century, but I think that is not entirely just, considering the money he paid for it was used for the essential preservation of the caves.

The chains of caves leading backwards into the cliff were dark and cool, the air smelt musty. Outside was hot and glaring bright, and the air was raining sand. As the wind gusted over the dunes on the cliff top, it fell in a gritty waterfall on the heads of people below. I'd washed my hair the previous evening, and now whenever I shook my head, sand ran down the back of my neck.

At lunchtime Ellen and I realised we had missed the bus back to town so we went to a local hotel where Chinese people are allowed to stay. The dining room was almost empty and although many more Chinese came after us, the waitresses ignored us and gave food to everyone else. When I'm hungry I get bad-tempered. Perhaps the staff hadn't understood our orders and had been afraid to lose face by bringing the wrong thing, but it happened frequently that Europeans were last to be served. I wondered if it's done to show us that although we are 'foreign friends' now we're still second-class world citizens, formerly barbarians. So I tried to keep my temper, went into the kitchen, pointed at what I wanted to eat, and waited there until a dish was provided. Ellen made me laugh (in a friendly, not malicious way) because she seemed never contented, and even when surrounded by fantastic frescoes she yearned to see a close-up view of the ceiling. We ate a hearty meal and she longed for other food. We climbed sand mountains and she wanted to see the one whose tip was above all the rest, never quite satisfied. Maybe that's what makes her travel.

To get back to Dunhwang we hitched a ride with a busload of Chinese factory workers from Lanzhou. With the caves' Buddhist images still fresh in my mind I asked my neighbour about his religious beliefs, explaining my question: here the people believed in Buddha, but the Moslems worship Allah, and my country is Christian, please tell what God you believe in. He pondered his answer for a moment then replied, 'I believe in the Communist Party'. In fact this seems to be a fairly universal Chinese attitude; the Party were promising an earthly paradise, and the Party took on the role of an all-caring father. It's only the Chinese who live outside their motherland in places like Singapore or Hong Kong who still hold religious beliefs, which are generally a mixture of ancestor-worship with Buddhism, Taoism and Confucianism.

The militant creed of Islam took hold of Xinjiang and elsewhere in northern China when it swept along the Silk Road in the 1300s. More recently, a steady flow of Christian missionaries devoted their lives to the mammoth task of converting the Chinese. But Christianity never really caught on. It's a foreign religion and was being spread by foreign devils. A Christian priest who spent twenty years in Kashgar made only one convert. One other man, a Polish exile from Siberia, used to go to his chapel services, but they finally quarrelled and the Pole was banned from the chapel. Unknown to the priest, he used to hear the services by kneeling with his ear to the chapel door.

Later that week I persuaded Ellen to come with me to Nan-hu, an oasis sixty miles from Dunhwang which had once been called 'Barrier of the Sun'. We boarded a public bus and after trundling through the desert for two hours the bus dropped us in a nowhere emptiness. The driver pointed to some hills about a mile from the road and said that was where we would find the 'Barrier of the Sun'. Despite the gruelling sun it was pleasant to be out walking. Soft sand dunes had given way to sharp outcrops of hard quartz pebbles which scrunched beneath our feet – red, rose-pink, russet, lilac, purple, maroon, black and yellow. We took an undulating route until we came to a deep canyon blocking the way. Numerous gulleys led part-way down and we slithered the rest, stopping only to work out where to cross the stream which snaked along the green corridor of the canyon base. We scrambled up into dry hills and eventually arrived at the ruined watchtower that marked the Barrier on the pass between the Lob Desert and the Tsaidam Basin, an important site in 100 BC, guarding the entrance to the southern arm of the Silk Road. It is a beautiful spot; beyond the multi-coloured quartz dunes were sand dunes and snowy mountains whose bases were lost in the heat haze. The vast plain beyond the barrier had been the site of Sachu city, though nothing now remains. To the west were a few distant oases, like green islands, their shores lapped by waves of shimmering haze. What excited me was knowing that beyond the horizon and on and on beyond lies only the desert, its secrets lost in its scorching, drifting sands. To stand gazing at its unconfined immensity brought a feeling of elation.

Ellen and I roamed around until heat and tiredness persuaded us to return to that stream we had crossed, and when we reached it we both stripped off to lie in the water. It was fast running, I held on to a root at the bank and let the current pull at me like a piece of trailing waterweed. Going upstream among poplar trees, purple bell flowers and small frogs that hopped out of our way we soon arrived at two lakes and the oasis of Nan-hu. Here at Nan-hu we met an old Chinese lady tottering along on tiny bound feet, and accepted her invitation to relax at her house. The house and courtyard were elegantly made of cool stone and plaster, and the main room had a raised platform with carpets and sleeping mats, and tidy piles of quilts. Her equally elderly husband, with a threadbare moustache and a toothless grin, said his name was Jan-shue-shei, and he was seventy-five. His wife, Ko-dengyi, was seventy-four. We all sat down to drink bowls of hot water and to nibble on steamed buns and folded bread which was filled with coloured powders.

Ko-dengyi asked me to stand up beside her to measure my height. I was head and shoulders taller. Then, taking me by the hand, she led me into another room to some family photographs. I felt so sorry about the way she hobbled along on those pathetically bound feet. You can never unbind the feet, which would become too painful without the supporting bandages. Apart from admiring the photographs I also noticed a couple of things which had probably come from the ruins of Suchow, found generations ago and still passed down among the locals. Common objects, a bowl and a comb, their usefulness unchanged. When I think of them in terms of the lives that wrought and used them, and brought them through to now, their familiar and homely images grow somewhat magnificent.

The old lady sent a message to tell the bus to call at her house, and when it arrived, hooting at us to hurry, we said hasty goodbyes and I gave her my postcard of the British Royal Family, which delighted her.

From Dunhwang, which is in Gansu province, I was aiming for the Gansu Corridor, a narrow, fertile strip of land between the Qilian Mountains and the desert of Inner Mongolia. At 6 a.m. I boarded the daily bus, ready for a ten-hour journey. The bus route led out past a string of tumbled watchtowers, spaced every *li* (kilometre). Dunhwang means blazing beacons, and these towers were used to send messages by fire-signal across the desert's empty spaces. There were occasional ruins of large fortified farmsteads, and two ruined strongholds with impressive gateways and corner-towers. Fortification was a way of life along this stretch of the Silk Road. For defence, some Gansu farmsteads had double or triple gateways and some forts had no doors. Access was either via a tunnel, or by being winched up in a basket on a rope. On reaching Jiayuguan I dumped my luggage at the hotel and hitch-hiked out to see the fort at the end of the Great Wall.

It seemed appropriate that I should get my first view of the Great Wall, which runs from the coast for 3,000 miles across China, at this furthest point inland. Not that much of it here is still standing, because this end was built of rammed earth, not stone. The crumbled remnants are only about fifteen feet high, with a thin pathway along the top. From the fort, a wall with several watchtowers leads across the barren sand to the base of Qilian Shan and a snowy range against a blue sky. It doesn't matter how often I see snow-capped mountains, there is always that tightening of the heart which comes from the remoteness of beauty that lies beyond my footsteps.

In the opposite direction, Mongolia was about thirty miles away. Where I stood in the Gansu Corridor's mouth a hot wind was blowing. It buried the base of the walls, scoured their sides and eroded the top. The fort itself has been greatly restored and is new and rather ugly, quite a disappointment, although some parts of the original fort still stand. Its ramparts are about thirty feet tall, and difficult to walk around because they don't all link up, while the outer entrapping ramparts and extra walls make it yet more confusing at ground level. Nowadays the entrance is through the Flood Gate. Once past that, it took me half an hour to find the arched main gate, the Gate of

Enlightenment, topped by a temple with red pillars. The thick metal doors beneath the arch were open. Inside the fort were many other tourists. The Chinese ones were busily taking pictures of each other, and it made me realise how my pictures are usually empty. The fort has two entrances, and the western one which opens into the Gobi is known as the Travellers' Gate. I recalled the stories of men exiled and expelled through that gate, outlaws, offenders, and disgraced officials, and I wondered about the feelings of the travellers who had passed willingly beneath it. According to Mildred Cable and Francesca French, the archway walls had been covered in graffiti. Now that the place is restored there's only a wooden notice saying 'No Carving or Writing'. And the gate is locked.

The Misses Cable and French had mentioned an ancient custom that any person leaving China through the Travellers' Gate would pause to throw a stone at the outer wall of the gatehouse. If the stone rebounded off the wall it meant that the person would return. If it fell flat, he might never return. To reach the outside of the gatehouse I had to trek around the outside of the fort and was surprised to find one part of the new brick façade had again been worn away into a hole, caused by new generations of modern Chinese still throwing stones to foretell their return. Many pebbles lay scattered on the ground so I picked one up and threw it. It rebounded, landing with a clinking noise on a heap of pebbles. But I wondered when I would come back.

The following morning brought one of the strangest breakfasts I've yet eaten. It was a bowl of rice gruel, a dish of cold sliced gherkin-like vegetable, a dish of raw grated onion, some peanuts (to be eaten with chopsticks), sugared tomatoes, and a cup of hot sweet milk. At 60 fen it wasn't expensive. (There are 100 fen to the yuan.) The kitchen boy said it was a typical Han breakfast. I got the feeling that I'd left Central Asia and now entered China.

8   Graves and warriors

About 320 miles east of the fort at the end of the wall, the Silk Road passes through Lanzhou and divides into branches for two destinations. The northern routes lead to Beijing and the southern route goes to Xian (formerly Chang'an), which used to be the capital of China. It had been one of the most splendid and cosmopolitan cities on earth.

I opted for this latter route and hitch-hiked as far as Lanzhou, getting a lift with a Han driver who kept telling me that China is a very backward country and apologising for it. The backwardness is surprising when one considers that up until the fourteenth century China had a clear technological superiority over Europe. The Chinese were also more advanced in civil engineering: roads, walls, bridges, hydraulic engineering, and they were the inventors of the compass for navigation. In astronomy, mathematics and economics, the Chinese also took the lead. Their first calendar predates the Western Julian calendar by eighty years. But the truck I sat in wasn't going to win any first prize. It belched thick exhaust which came up through the flooring, and the clouds of exhaust outside got blown forward by the wind at the same speed as the Han was driving. Thus we sat in a total smog.

The Han had such a strong regional accent that I could hardly understand a word he said. Our conversation was a guessing game, with me guessing what he was talking about. When I asked him what cargo his truck carried he pointed to some bits of paper. It wouldn't be a load of milled paper – there are not enough trees in the Gobi for paper-making; perhaps some other ingredient or chemical for paper. Among their technological achievements the Chinese invented paper, in AD 100–200. They were the inventors of printing and developed a currency of paper money; as well as printing the world's first book, they were the originators of dictionaries and encyclopaedias. All these ideas flowed to Europe along the Silk Road.

Next morning I braced myself for an early assault on the Chinese railway system again. To board trains the Chinese do form queues but these tend to degenerate into a crushing mob as the train stops. They elbow their way to be first aboard,

leaving no space for passengers to get off. The guard barred
the door and yelled at the mob to get back into line. Three times
he forced us back into order, but whenever the door was opened
for people to disembark, the line hurled itself forwards. It
seemed ludicrous to me, but I suppose that if you are one of a
billion people you soon learn that if you don't jump the queue
you'll not find a seat. Needless to say, I couldn't find one. So I
walked through the train until a man moved up to make room
for me. He could speak French fairly fluently, and told me that
he had spent three years in Algiers, working in the Chinese
Embassy. Suddenly he blurted out in French, 'You foreigners
are all rich people while we Chinese are poor. Our workers
earn 50 yuan (£17) a month. What do yours earn?' I couldn't
deny there's a vast difference, but I wanted to make him
understand that the cost of living is equally different. The rent
for an ordinary Chinese town house is only about one yuan per
month. It isn't reasonable to make a broad comparison. The
type of tourist seen here is usually wealthy because tours to
China are expensive, while a traveller may have a small budget.
But I didn't envy the first-class passengers, their journeys might
be very boring. Whenever the train stopped at a station and
scores of people boarded there were more violent outbursts as
they squabbled over getting seats. It seemed rather like being
on the roosting poles of a chicken house, the chickens flapping
and squawking in their efforts to find space to perch.

Outside, the hillsides were steeply terraced with scalloped
paddy fields shaped to fit each contour. The crop season was
becoming more advanced as we went south; we left behind the
flooded greens and watched the rice growing heavy with grain.
On mountain promontories I noticed a couple of ruined castles,
and later in sandy *loess* cliffs I caught sight of many man-made
caves which were people's dwellings, some with front doors.

Several of the people wandering through the carriage stopped
to say hello to me. One brought his English language book and
he wanted me to give him an English lesson. So I let him read
aloud while I corrected wrong pronunciations and explained
the difficult words. The stories in his book were taken from
Chinese everyday life woven with propaganda, one story being
about a shop assistant who says, 'My work may sound boring,
but I'm proud to be doing my bit to help with the four moderni-
sations of the Party.' Modernisation is the new Chinese goal,
and one no longer hears Mao's slogans. I'd not even seen a
copy of Mao's Little Red Book.

At 11 p.m. the train reached Xian. The hotel which normally offers student prices was full and they could only offer me a room for 50 yuan (£17), ten times more than I usually paid. This being above my budget allowance, I began searching for another hotel. After two that would not accept me because I was a foreigner, I found a hostel which was again expensive at 30 yuan. It was now past midnight, rather late to be walking around in a city looking for a hotel. And it was raining. The clerk was uncooperative but the second time I went back she offered me a shared room for 18 yuan. The Hong Kong girl I shared it with had only paid 9 yuan, being Chinese. Most prices in this region seem to be raised for foreigners.

In the morning my room-mate told me, 'If you've seen real temples in China, you won't enjoy seeing Xian's reproductions. They are not living things.' I took her advice and avoided all but two places that I particularly wanted to see. The first site was Ban Po, a neolithic village which dates back to 5000 BC. The four levels of the dig cover generations of different cultures and at the deepest level are mementoes of wild nomads who became settled. This region may be considered the cradle of Chinese civilisation; it has been inhabited since pre-neolithic times, and the first civilised states recorded in China were here over 3000 years ago.

The neolithic women of Ban Po are said to have invented agriculture, using the slash and burn method to cultivate millet. They used stone axes set in wooden hafts, and developed mill-wheels and grinding-stones. Men were occupied with hunting, using three-pronged spears, and fishing, and then came the domestication of animals, including dogs. The Ban Po women produced practical coiled clay pottery. The kilns which have been excavated show temperatures reached of 1,000°F. With this skill they became sedentary people. Women also learned to sew with bone needles, and to weave and spin using spinning whorls and bone shuttles. Their textiles were hemp, rattan and animal hair. Technology had been set in motion. At one stage the village had a matriarchal society; when they developed a primitive form of money they began using a calculation aid of twenty-two different carved symbols. These were the predecessors of the script on tortoise-shells from the Shang dynasty, the earliest writing known in China.

The excavated skeletons had been buried all facing in one direction, and many had burial objects, which tends to imply a belief in afterlife. One young girl of only three or four had been buried with eighty funerary objects, bone beads, stone balls and jars. The excavated mud and straw huts are of a later date, but quite sophisticated, with tunnel entrances for protection against the weather, and raised earthen bed platforms like one still sees today. Public food-storage pits denote a communal approach, while private cellars show private ownership, dividing the rich from the poor and producing a class system. The moat around the village was twenty-five feet deep and archaeologists had calculated that its excavation would have amounted to 3670 truckloads of earth. That made me smile because I'd yet to see earth being carried in trucks; usually it was in hand carts or donkey carts.

The only other site I wanted to visit was the excavation of the famous terracotta army, 6,000 lifesize clay soldiers, grouped in battle order. This has attracted the world's notice since it was discovered only ten years ago. The figures stand in ranks, many of the infantry hold swords or crossbows, some archers kneel in the firing position, faces intent on their aim, and there are several horse-drawn chariots with charioteers. The army is believed to guard a royal tomb, but no tomb has yet been discovered in the immediate vicinity. A guide said that the tomb builders and craftsmen of the terracotta army had been killed and buried in pits nearby so that they could never tell about the tomb's location. What a waste of manpower and of art. The skill of their pottery shows in every small sculpted detail – fingernails, moustaches, beards, individual hairstyles; some warriors have their long hair in a bun to one side of their head. Others wear various types of hats and caps, belted tunics, armoured suits, short boots and square curly-toed shoes. But it is their faces and varying expressions that give each one its personality. If I closed my mind to the other tourists it could have been a ghostly place. Restoration and excavation are still going on. The restoration is extensive and painstaking. At the back end of each excavated line of ranks there are ranks of partially excavated warriors, seeming to be growing from the ground, only their head and shoulders sticking out. Some of the vertical dig-walls have clay arms and shoulders sprouting sideways out of the earth.

Later that day I met a Danish historian and we discussed the destructive forces of China's more recent past. The last thirty years have brought massive political upheavals, homicidal purges, and violent idealism that backfired in the Great Leap

Forward and the Cultural Revolution. The Dane was trying to convince me that Mao was China's greatest destructive power. The Cultural Revolution was a terrifying thing. It wiped out over half of the country's elite. Several million professional people, administrators, managers, petty officials, scientists, academics, school teachers, anyone who held a position of authority, and those who had capitalist or bourgeois sentiments, were generally imprisoned, persecuted or killed under 'counter-revolutionary' charges. The Red Guards were given official blessing to tear down the old system, get rid of the country's past, and clear a space for a new future. They did it by terror and destruction for eleven years. This was the Dane's case. True, this cannot be condoned, but one should give Mao some credit for helping the peasants to overthrow a suffocating bureaucracy. Administrators had held such power (being simultaneously the law-enforcer, magistrate and tax-collector) that corruption was inevitable and they became greedy and tyrannical. But the landlords didn't suffer because they simply taxed the peasants more heavily. The peasants were bled beyond the brink of starvation.

Despite the present-day discrediting of Mao's theories, and in some cases the complete reversal of his policies, he has not been much devalued. Some of his doctrines were so contradictory that people say they're still in use, having been re-interpreted. Emperors always got total loyalty, and Mao was no different. If Mao said 'Plant rice' the people planted rice, chopping down fruit orchards and deforesting the land to make room for more. And for the unjustly persecuted people who survived the ordeal, there is now reinstatement with honour. Nowadays the new Party policies seem 'counter-revolutionary', allowing free market enterprise, foreign investment, profits, cash bonuses, advertising, and an open door to the West. But they have no reputation for stability. It made me glad to live at a time when China accepts individual travellers. But Xian wasn't a place where I wanted to linger. The northern arm of the Silk Road goes to Beijing. Marco Polo was headed that way. So was I, though I planned to stop over in a part of the Gobi between Inner Mongolia and the Yellow River.

While eating supper that evening, I watched the Chinese bolting their food, mouths low over their plates and concentrating only on feeding themselves as quickly as possible. This is normal; people don't usually talk at table, they eat as if there's no tomorrow. Perhaps they'll never forget the hungry times or maybe they fear that hunger lies ahead. The Chinese have a saying, 'Every grain of rice that you leave in your bowl will be a tear that you shed before the day is out.'

9 Bicycle philosophy

Leaving Xian, the railway line ran alongside the Wei River, a major tributary of the Yellow River or Hwang Ho. Its colour was a very muddy yellow, and here it flowed through steep knobbly mountains whose peaks were lost in cloud. The river was often shallow with rocks, but it looked easily runnable by canoe. There were no boats, nor much habitation. A long calm gorge again turned my thoughts to canoeing, but I was pleased to change my mind when the calm gorge suddenly ended in a steep and massive dam waterfall.

The Wei River – I looked for its name meaning in my dictionary: depending on the tone used it can mean to smell or taste (I think not), another *wei* means hello (used on the telephone), or it can be a guard. The man sitting beside me said it is none of those, it is just a name. I wanted to argue that most Chinese names have meanings, but didn't since if I was right it would make my neighbour lose face. He was a doctor and spoke quite good English. He told me that he'd once invited foreign friends to stay at his house, but on the second day the police came and told them to move. The other person on our seat was a boy who had just failed his university entrance exam. It meant that his life now had zero opportunity of modern improvement, he would have to work at farming. He was silent and depressed.

The train went through a series of tunnels as we progressed along the gorge. With every tunnel, black sooty smoke poured into the carriages through the open windows. We emerged from the gorge into barren mud hills, greenness receded and was replaced by desert. At noon I went to the crowded dining car and bought some boiled rice, chicken, and fungus. Black fungus, large flabby bits and little concave buttons, the flavours weren't strong and they tasted good. The chicken I left untouched. My serving had been two sets of feet and claws, and a scraggy neck.

Outside the window, the desert rolled past. We entered Ningxia Autonomous Region, a province of desert bordering Mongolia. Ningxia has only been open to foreigners for ten months, but few people bother to stop because they would lose their seat or sleeper on the train; or because they have no time left on their visa and are hurrying to Beijing and out of China. An Australian joined me for a while; he was in a hurry to reach Beijing and catch the Trans-Siberian Express back to Europe. While he sat by me, none of the Chinese spoke to me or tried to make friends. One of the advantages of going solo is the way that local people accept you among them. Xenophobia has always been a characteristic of China. It's impressive how dramatically their attitude has changed in the last seven years. The Great Wall, which I glimpsed several times during this train ride, was built to keep out 'foreign devils'. All foreigners were considered to be barbarians. China had wanted nothing to do with them; there was no reason why such a mighty country should be interested in the vile and depraved deeds of foreigners. Her borders were closed. She remained remarkably isolated until the world powers forced her into trade concessions in the 1800s. The anti-foreign hatred with its spy-mania and harassment of Europeans was rife until only about seven years ago. Now China has an open-door business policy but it is a one-way door. They don't want to buy our products, they only want our technical expertise and our machinery so that they can produce the goods for themselves. Suddenly now we're the 'foreign friends'. Though we normally get no preferential treatment and sometimes the authorities seem to delight in thwarting our plans. Many times when I've asked for permits they've been refused, and the phrase 'it's not convenient' is familiar to all China-travellers.

The train route through Ningxia follows the giant northerly loop of the Yellow River. The rice produced here is famous throughout China. The Yellow River is also known for its disastrous floods. In Chinese folklore there are various great flood legends. Some tell of an immense inundation so deep it covered the hills, leaving only two or three people in makeshift boats. The Norsu group of south-west China (whom I hoped to visit later on) claim to be descended from Noah and his three sons who survived the flood. Chinese Noah (Fu-hsi) was another character, recorded in 2200 BC when the Yellow River flooded the land for nine years.

Yinchuan, where I left the train, is the provincial capital of Ningxia and the Hui who inhabit Ningxia are a minority group of staunch Moslems. Some of their women wear white veils over the back of their heads, with tunics and black baggy trousers, while the men wear Chinese Mao clothes and coolie hats. Yinchuan city seems to be made up of many villages joined together by a new town, modernising fast. Almost all the concrete buildings have been constructed in the last six years. Much construction was still going on. My hotel was in the process of building new wings, and cartloads of modern reinforced concrete pillars were being pulled along by time-honoured donkey power.

On the roads there was little motorised traffic, and it didn't seem to have any road sense. Drivers came out of side-turnings at speed without looking, and those on the main road were continually blasting their air horns. Pedestrians didn't bother to hurry out of the way, despite the gruesome street-posters illustrating in gory colour what happens in accidents. It seems they've learned not to fear motor traffic.

The special stone product of this town is Helan Stone (from a nearby mountain) which is popularly carved into ornaments. It's a mud-stone of sedimentary rock, settled in uneven layers of black on pale green. The skill of the carver is to pick out a relief design in green on black.

I found a number of mosques and, it being Friday evening, there was a small stream of mostly elderly men making their way to pray, carrying their beads. As in Xinjiang, I noticed a fairly relaxed attitude to religious observances among the Moslems of Yinchuan. You certainly did not see them stopping work to pray five times a day, as in stricter parts of the Arab world.

At dinner I met a Canadian teacher under contract for a year at Yinchuan university. He was feeling a little frustrated with the system and said that at times he felt like a prisoner. He'd just been refused permission to buy a bicycle. With hindsight he realised that he should not have asked for permission; if he had simply gone out and bought one nobody would have seriously objected. The thing he found most irritating was that his students were not allowed to visit him alone, they had to be in groups, and his friendships had been stopped by the authorities warning the people concerned to stay away from him. Maybe our decadent Western ways would be contagious.

I wanted to ask the police if I could make side trips out of town, but the police station looked closed and abandoned, so I decided that it should be all right provided I returned before nightfall. The Canadian had mentioned some ancient beehive tombs in the desert about twenty miles away in a place about which little is known and in the morning I found a local bus which was going in the right direction. The tombs belonged to the Western Xia emperors of the eleventh century. Glazed clay tiles depicted peasants at work, horses and camels at rest. At their peak they were using coins, gold leaf, fine porcelain dishes and in the town museum I'd seen a ceremonial crown of delicately-wrought metal shaped into birds and snakes, set on a headband with many strings of metal beads hanging from it. An impressive item. The tombs are scattered over a vast area and I only managed to reach three of them. One has the remains of a walled enclosure, and on all three the exterior brickwork is eroded into deep crevices full of nesting birds. The ground is littered with broken fragments of pottery. I suppose that one day the place will be commercialised for tourists, but I felt privileged to have seen it before that time arrived.

Wandering around slowly absorbing the atmosphere I went further than I had intended; distance is deceptive in the clear desert light, and looking at my watch I realised that the last bus from the village to Yinchuan had probably left. Making haste across the scrubby desert I headed for the road, only a few miles away, hoping that when I reached it something might come along and give me a ride. In the time it took to walk there I didn't miss any rides; there was no traffic. For half an hour the only sign of life was a man riding a donkey with a spare donkey trotting behind. I asked if I could ride the spare donkey. He agreed, and gave me a bit of sacking to sit on. Even so, it was terribly uncomfortable, the donkey's back was easiest sat on right at the back of its rump and as it trotted along I worried that I'd get bounced off. Where the donkey-man took a side turning from the road I said goodbye and continued on foot.

A walking-tractor came along the road, the type of two-wheeled engine which pulls a cart; it was pulling a load of gravel. The driver gave me a lift on top of the gravel for about two miles until he turned off the road. I was still twelve miles from Yinchuan and the time was 7 p.m. I wondered what time supper would end at my hotel. I had been looking forward to tempting my jaded appetite with a good dinner. The empty road stretched straight across the desert up into the mountains bordering Inner Mongolia. A truck came into sight but so far away that it took a long time to reach me. It passed me without stopping. 'Ah well, you can't win them all,' I thought and plodded onward. Finally a man on a bicycle came past and without being asked he stopped. We walked and talked for a while before he suggested that I sit on the back carrier and let him pedal me back to Yinchuan, where he was going anyway.

Twelve miles seemed too far to allow someone to pedal carrying me but I agreed to take up his offer until I could stop a truck or something faster. He was already carrying his three-year-old son on the crossbar, and a basket containing eggs on the handlebars. I hoped that his kindness wouldn't be his downfall.

As he pedalled along we talked; he could speak English and was a school teacher, teaching history, geography and politics. Political studies are an important part of the school curriculum, though slightly less dominant than formerly, and marks are awarded for attitude, and not only for results. A student's poor attitude to his work can cost him dearly. He explained to me that 'individuals' and 'rebels' are not admired by their classmates, who rather see rebelliousness as a threat to their group security. The rebels are made to feel isolated from the group, and the group is their way of life. Right from junior school the children learn that conformity keeps you out of trouble. It makes them docile and obedient. The kindergarten takes over the role of a parent, teaching infants how to brush their teeth and taking care that their every moment is filled with organised activities. Throughout school life there will be activities, leaving no time for loafing around and wandering the streets. It's easy to keep tabs on individuals through the neighbourhood and street committees, whose concern is people's welfare. If they feel that a youngster is turning delinquent they will report it, to give the boy a chance to reform. It's seen as being for his own good. In school the focus is on teaching people to live in society, to be content with their fate, and to help others. Security means belonging to a unit, at your place of study, work, or service. People who don't have a unit are hardly noticed or recognised. With a unit, they become committed to that unit's security and they work together to keep it stable and prosperous.

The road ran through rice paddies, walled villages and bits of new industrial areas under construction. The bicycle's back carrier was more uncomfortable than the donkey had been; though I sat side-saddle there was nowhere to rest my feet, and the road was bumpy. My skill at balancing was nil and I was afraid to start shifting around in case it caused a disaster. The child sat quiet and docile. After sunset, still pedalling along and talking, the teacher told me something of his own past. He had been born and raised by the ocean, had lived at home with his family, and after schooling had qualified as a teacher. During the Cultural Revolution he was denounced as 'bourgeois' and he had been sent to till the fields beyond Yinchuan, these same rice paddies through which he now pedalled with me. He talked reluctantly about the Cultural Revolution, when the school children had formed Red Guard youth movements and attacked their nearest prey, their teachers. Breakdown of discipline gave them the go-ahead to disobey, insult, intimidate, shove around and physically assault the teachers. No wonder the schools had to close.

'For five years I slaved on these rice paddies. How I hate this place.' He had been reinstated as a teacher, but he had no thought of moving back to the coast, unable to leave the area. To apply for permission to leave would show him as not appreciating the Party line. And he was puzzled by my question about where he would choose to live since such a choice was never likely to be open to him. When we reached the suburbs of Yinchuan he dropped me at a bus stop; he was embarrassed by my thanks and because other people stood by listening he whispered his goodbyes and left hurriedly. By the time I reached the hotel it was 9.30 p.m. and it was certain that I'd missed dinner. Just to make sure I went into the kitchen and talked to one of the waitresses, who led me into the private dining area. There had been a party of officials in town and they'd had a sumptuous banquet, with such plentiful dishes that many had been left untouched on the tables. The waitress cleared a table for me and brought over some rice and full dishes of deep fried fish, tomatoes, cucumber and wolf-berries which are sweet and juicy like cherries with a knobbly skin. And afterwards she brought me a glass of port. When it came to paying for my share of the banquet, she charged me 80 fen. What a treat.

10   Along the Yellow River

From Yinchuan I backtracked to the small town of Zhong Wei, still in Ningxia and on the Yellow River, where I hoped for a chance to use my canoe. Zhong Wei is more isolated than Yinchuan, and I could tell how seldom individual travellers come here because of the way the local people grunted sharply with surprise and alarm at first seeing me. The town is small and pleasant with an old and shabbily beautiful drum tower at the meeting point of its four axial roads. As I wandered around, a Chinese man came over to introduce himself, and began a conversation. Misunderstanding one of his questions about my profession, I discovered that I'd inadvertently said I am a teacher. He said he was also a teacher and asked me politely if I would agree to give a lecture in simple English at the local school, though he apologised that the pupils were mostly peasant children. It would have been churlish to refuse, so we made a date for later in the week.

At the hotel a man explained in pantomime that at 8 p.m. there would be a performing ape on show. He slapped his chest and jumped around rubbing his shoulders as a demonstration. But when he said it in Chinese I was puzzled and tried for a new interpretation of his behaviour. It transpired he meant that if I wanted a shower, there would be some hot water at 8 p.m. Much better than a circus act.

In the morning I decided to reconnoitre a bit of the Yellow River. With the memory of falling out of the canoe still fresh in my mind I didn't want to be caught unawares by rapids on something the size of the Yellow River. So I arranged to hire a jeep and was accompanied by a very helpful representative of CITS (China International Travel Service) called Chen. On the way Chen wanted to show me a stretch of the Great Wall, but we had trouble finding it. On reaching a long low bank of rammed earth my companion blinked a few times and ex- claimed: 'But a year ago the Great Wall was intact here!' All we could see was a bank of foundations and some villagers shovelling earth into wheelbarrows, taking it away to make into bricks for new houses. While walking along the hump of its foundations, I picked up a coin, an old Chinese coin with a square hole in it. Chen said it dated from the Xing dynasty when a woman was queen of the Hans.

From there we drove through orchards and scrubland, which had formerly been desert, reclaimed by modern techniques – the positive side of progress. We were heading for a desert reclamation project where a group of scientists and peasants were working on schemes to control desert encroachment. I was interested to see how the Chinese are tackling the problem. One technique, used extensively along railway embankments, is a quilt of straw squares to stop the sand covering the track. The local people must appreciate the project since they do not allow their camels to destroy the straw squares. They are also experimenting with chemicals to harden the sand, and with dry earth tolerating shrubs and trees, planted to start building up enough soil to merit irrigation and subsequent cultivation.

The following day I explored the area a little more closely by camel. It was a small camel, somewhat thin with humps flopped over and rather bald, having shed its winter coat. And hungry – it kept snatching mouthfuls from every bush we passed; the variety of different leaves it liked was considerable. But I didn't encourage it to stop and eat because the trees were part of the desert reclamation project. The camel's control was via a nosepeg and one rope, making right turns easy, and left turns impossible without going in circles. After a few miles I began to regret not having insisted on using a saddle.

Sand dunes loomed in the distance like mountains. Their foothills were golden yellow crescent-shaped dunes, stretching for miles. My camel plodded slowly, the only times he moved fast were on the down-slopes of the dunes. His flat furry feet didn't seem adapted for hills. From a high point overlooking the Yellow River I could see how it loops its winding course. The camel's owner appeared behind us, riding another camel just as scrawny as mine. After a short while we came to a mud hovel where we paused to rest. The camel's owner pointed to the remnants of a wall and said that this was once a big Mongolian village, used by them as a market to barter their sheep, camels and cattle for staple foodstuffs from the Hui and Han.

The Mongolians still come here every year, to winter in Zhong Wei, bringing their circular white yurts and setting up near town. In spring they head out for pasturelands 180 miles away. Before we left, a Mongolian with three laden camels arrived from the town; he had stayed behind for health treatment and was now going to join his mates. He wore a long black coat, sash, and a duck-cap which had a birdlike beak and a button to hold it up. When we left I asked my companion if my camel has a name. He looked at me blankly and said why should it want a name, it's a camel. Though he added that in Mandarin they also call a camel a sand-boat (*sha-mua*).

It was not until the following day that I found a suitable place to launch my canoe on to the Yellow River. When I was down at water level the river looked bigger and far more powerful than I'd previously realised but at this stage it had no sizeable rapids or stopper holes, just a swirling flat torrent of yellow-brown water. My put-in place was on the inside of a bend. A camel watched me make ready the canoe and I waved goodbye to it as I paddled out into the current. Inside the bend the current was spinning back on itself, it was hard to make progress but after about thirty strokes I bounced over the trough demarcation between up- and down-stream currents, and was away at speed.

The mainstream looked the roughest but its turbulence was neglible, it was the awesome strength of the thick yellow muddy current that impressed me. A big river by any standards, its total length is over 3000 miles, and it waters a basin twice the size of France. The current carried me around the outside bank as the river looped its way in a series of S-bends through craggy hills and mountainous sand dunes. One bend had a landslide of purple rock in its yellow dunes. On the flatter, low-lying inner bends were cultivated plots of rice and poplar trees, but not yet any villages. A mile or so further there was a village on the south bank. Stopping just before it, I left my canoe pulled up on to the shore, and went for a walkabout to stretch my legs. Leading from the village southwards was a massive old earthen wall, still in parts wide and strong enough for me to walk along its crumbling top. It led across desert and into dark distant mountains. Its northern end turned a right-angled corner near the village and ran behind it to the east. It was of such size and age that I asked some people if it is part of the Great Wall, and they assured me that indeed it is. The people have made use of it in a different way, by hollowing caves into its thickness which are used as pigpens and night stables for other stock.

From around every corner crowds of people began materialising. It seemed that the whole village had come to stare at me, even the school children came rushing from their classrooms, their teachers in hot pursuit, not to order them back to class but to get the chance of saying good morning and practising their English. They told me that there is no bridge across the river in this region, though it is easily crossed by boat or ferry in summer. In winter the ice used to be thick enough for trucks to drive across it. But about three years ago a change in the climate has meant the ice is now usually too thin for safe crossings.

Back on the river the current began to get swirlier and demanded my concentration. The past two bends had contained sandbanks with rapid shallows, though they weren't proper rapids, for which I felt thankful. My attention was caught by some giant water wheels, forty foot in diameter. Their wooden spokes, green with weed, made stark dark silhouettes in motion. The water is raised in their bamboo tubes and emptied at the top of the wheel's arc into a sequence of wooden troughs sloping down toward the paddies which they irrigate. Cheap power but not very effective, much of the water falling from the wheels missed the aqueducts and came pouring back into the river. The villagers said they repair the wheels annually but the wood is so decrepit that they really need replacing. Perhaps they would be replaced by a motor-driven water pump.

I should have liked to stay in one of the riverbank villages for the night, but this is forbidden to foreigners. The problem is not so much that you'd be in trouble with the authorities, but that your hosts would be punished in some way. So I returned to Zhong Wei and put in my normal appearance at dinner in the hotel – half a fish, rice and a sugared omelette. The major domo wouldn't let me sit with the Chinese. On the first day when I had joined them he had asked me to move. So I sat at a table on my own, and felt uncomfortable about it. Five tables of people stared at me. I had been given a knife and fork; perhaps that was why everyone stared. No, it's because they always stare. I was still having difficulty adjusting to accept these manners as normal. Different things are polite and impolite, one can be impolite without knowing by making someone lose face; and things which are impolite to me, such as staring, mean nothing in their culture.

The next morning I went downriver to Mud Ho, the delightfully named village where I had been told they used inflated skin rafts. Sure enough there were several rafts propped up in the shade on the riverbank. An old Han called Lee took me for a ride downriver. His raft was made of inflated sheepskins in four rows by four long, all tied underneath a flimsy wooden frame of crosspoles. It was surprisingly stable and comfortable. The skins were pudgy rather than hard-inflated, smooth leather. Each skin in these rafts has many small knots closing each orifice; neck, tail and four legs, and it is inflated through one of the legs. New skins are a semi-translucent, pale tan colour, and they last about three years depending on how often the raft is used. When a skin develops a blackish coating it is time to throw it away because old skins get waterlogged and heavy. Lee was on his way to collect two new skins. We put in at a sandy beach, the current tugged quickly at the raft and away we went. Lee used a long heavy wooden paddle, taking us midriver into the fast current and settling down to relax.

Another raft set out from the opposite shore, aiming to cross the river, providing a ferry service. This small raft carried six passengers, some full sacks and a bicycle. Lee said that it's not infrequent for a raft to capsize. But there's no great danger provided you can hold on to the raft, which cannot sink. The golden brown water looked like thick soup, with strong eddies. One spun the raft in a circle but Lee re-aligned it with ease. The riverbanks here were uninhabited; the northern one was a gravel sweep backed by a flat low plain with rice paddies, while opposite was sand and gravel rising to craggy barren mountains.

I played around paddling the raft for a while, it wasn't nearly as manoeuvrable as my canoe. But it was much more stable. Finally we pulled into an eddy, paddling hard against the current, and glided into the shore. When I asked Lee how he would take the raft upriver he said that it was not at all heavy, he would just carry it on his shoulders.

Later on I met Chen again. I got the impression that I knew more about his region than he did, since when I told him about the stretch of Great Wall I'd found, he asked for its location so he could take future tourists there, and when I mentioned the water wheels, he said he'd lived in Zhong Wei for twenty years and never knew that they existed. He reminded me that I had agreed to give a lecture at the school before I left. I had been trying not to think about that.

In the classroom I was confronted by fifty students sitting at their desks. 'Good evening,' I said. 'Good evening,' they all chorused. My chosen topics were geography and history, and I had been warned not to make any political statements nor say anything that could be criticised as 'Western propaganda'. But

I felt that the subjects were less important than the fact of hearing English spoken by an English person; it's hard to learn just from books and written exercises. The students were very shy about responding to my questions though their teachers encouraged them from the back of the classroom. Occasionally an answer would be shouted through from outside the open door and windows. It was after school hours and about 200 other pupils (presumably the rest of the school) had come voluntarily, and were crammed together outside listening.

11 Grandmother's footsteps

I arrived in Beijing late one evening, booked into a hotel, and spent a few days adjusting to the city on a bicycle. Most of Beijing's traffic is bicycles; the morning rush hour is a thick, seemingly solid pedalling column. Turning right is simple because you ignore the traffic signals and slide off to the right. But turning left can be a nightmare when you're stuck in the middle of a major thoroughfare with trolley buses turning left around you. I tended to wait until another cyclist wanted to turn, and go at the same time. Accidents are common, but usually it's cyclists that bump into each other and they fall over unhurt. I caused quite a pile-up myself when a cyclist saw me and fell off his bike. People stare at me just as much here as in other places. Their black-haired sameness is in fact made up of individually different faces. But they don't smile.

Some women have modern hairstyles, and are developing a taste for fashionable clothes. Beauty used to be a disadvantage, but now people are waking up to it being all right to look nice. Children wear bright colours, and the trousers of all Chinese babies are split open along the centre seam – it's a practical alternative to nappies, though during President Reagan's recent visit to Beijing, mothers were asked to sew up their children's trouser splits in case the tradition was seen as indecent.

In the very early morning I went to watch old people practising *t'ai chi chuan* in the coal-smoggy parks and in the middle of flowery roundabouts. *T'ai chi chuan* is supposed to re-connect your body with the air's natural energy through controlled breathing and ritual shadow-boxing exercises. More familiarly, innumerable joggers panted past. It seems to have caught on among all ages as popularly as in the USA. In another area people were singing operatic songs and playing musical instruments, each on his or her own, not regarding each other and all playing different songs. The cacophonous result was slightly mind-boggling but made sense when I realised that they're just doing their own thing.

I had sufficient exercise on the bicycle. Beijing is huge and I must have pedalled twenty miles a day. Within the old Tartar city walls of Beijing were the walls of the Imperial City and beside these the walled Forbidden City, built in the 1400s. The emperors seldom went outside, and no one entered the Forbidden City without permission. The isolated inner palace was where the emperors had sat on the Dragon Throne, surrounded by unimaginable luxury.

I walked from end to end of the Forbidden City, detouring to see rock-gardens and temples, lured on by names like the Gate of Heavenly Purity, Gate of Earthly Tranquillity, the Hall of Supreme Harmony, Palace of Abstinence, Palace of Culture of the Mind, Palace of Peace and Longevity, and Palace of Accumulated Elegance. It's only in fairly recent years that the Forbidden City has been opened to tourists. My mother, who was born in Hankow and raised in Beijing, had never been able to look inside. From a hillock in the outer Imperial City which was open to the public, she told me how she used to look out over the Forbidden City, seeing it derelict, falling down yet still so sacrosanct that no one could enter it. She could tell the emperor's halls because green-tiled roofs signified ordinary places, while gold tiles meant imperial. Beijing's only blue-tiled building was the Temple of Heaven. As I walked through the centre of the Forbidden City I could see the top of the hill where she must have stood. I was inside looking out, though I was one of hundreds of tourists in there. None of them was European (it was midday and the package tours were probably resting), but there were many hundreds of provincial Chinese, holiday-makers in Mao-style clothes. Mao was on the Long March and helping the communists to fight the Kuomintang in the days when my mother lived in China (1924–37) during the era of the warlords. She said that fighting had seemed frequent in the provinces, and armies came and went from Beijing but she was too young to know whose armies they were, except that they belonged to the warlords. 'And if our rickshaws took us along the Glacis Road when executions were going on, our nanny told us to look the other way.'

My grandmother, Doris Beddow, saw it differently:

July 6, 1928.
Things have been quiet since the Shansi warlord moved into Peking, though the retreating Fengtien army's stragglers have been robbing and molesting road users. The city gates stayed closed for two days, the Post Office van didn't arrive in time and was locked out. The southern Shansi army seem courteous, but we stay alert for outbreaks of rioting; our

valuables have gone into storage, the cook can't find fish for sale, and there are some shortages; the daily delivery of ice has been late. [Ice was cut off lakes and canals in winter and packed under earth mounds, in storage for selling in summer. Their winter coal was delivered by camels that had walked from Manchuria.]

Tennis and polo have proceeded without interruption. Though rickshaws and cars travelling after 9 p.m. are frequently stopped. The Shansi soldiers are countryfolk with ragged uniforms. Ancient brass guns mounted on pack mules serve as artillery. But the men have pleasant smiles and polite manners, which is a refreshing contrast to the behaviour of the Fengtien soldiers.

Marco Polo, his father and uncle ended their epic journey in 1273 when they reached the emperor's summer palace near Beijing, and soon after my own arrival in Beijing I made my way there by public bus. The emperor, Kublai Khan, received the Polos honourably and graciously; he was impressed with the Holy Oil but more than that, he was pleased by the journeys that the Polos had made on his behalf. When he asked about the young stranger's identity (Marco was now twenty-one), Marco's father answered 'That is your servant and my son.'

'In Xanadu did Kubla Khan a stately pleasure dome decree . . .' Coleridge's poem was about this summer palace, inspired by reading Marco Polo's book. Temples and pagodas lie along a lakeshore, whose inlets are spanned by ornamental bridges and whose tranquil blue waters are dotted with water-lilies, swans and a flotilla of small pleasure boats. All-powerful, the Mongol emperor Kublai Khan reigned two decades after the first great Mongol emperor, Ghengiz Khan, whose armies had conquered the lands from north China to the Crimea. In those two decades the Mongol armies continued conquering westward through Hungary, Poland, and reached within a hundred miles of Berlin. Only the death of the army leader, Ghengiz's son Ogotai, prevented them reaching France and England. Under Kublai Khan China prospered; the Silk Road re-opened and the empire flourished.

Marco Polo's arrival here was not the end of his journey, it was the beginning of seventeen years' travelling as an imperial emissary. He had earned the Khan's respect by his quick mastery of four languages, and on his official fact-finding missions for the emperor he behaved with such wisdom and prudence that he was showered with honours. I was looking forward to picking up his trail again later in western and south-west China. As the Polos had paid their respects to their great benefactor, I called on mine. I have the good fortune to share a surname with an old established hong or China trading company, the House of Dodwell. We are not related – it was only my mother's family which lived in Beijing, not my father's. Nevertheless Dodwell International, as they now are, generously bought me the plane ticket to Urumchi which started off my journey, and entertained me handsomely in Beijing. As traders in silk and tea their own beginnings in China flourished, appropriately I felt, as a direct result of a boat trip up the Yangtse by one of their directors in 1852. He had tried to make contacts for Dodwell's in this prime silk-producing region, but was promptly sent packing as a foreign devil. Disappointed by his mission's failure, he caught the return boat downriver, but during that night a typhoon blew up and it pushed the boat all the way back to the silk centre. In port the following morning the Englishman was approached by a delegation of elders and silk merchants. They had seen an omen in the typhoon, a message that spirits were offended by their refusal to have dealings with the foreigner. So to amend the damage, they offered him plentiful silk supplies on good terms. As a result of that river journey, Dodwell & Co. became firmly established in Shanghai, and it had a motto: 'A pessimist is he who sees a difficulty in every opportunity: an optimist is he who sees an opportunity in every difficulty.'

They certainly had their difficulties, retreating to Hong Kong during the Second World War and when China closed its doors. They have re-emerged in China now handling exports of textiles and imports of office machinery and general goods. Foreigners are not allowed to deal direct with Chinese factories, they must use a Chinese middle man who is chosen by the Party and who, in effect, controls the company's business there. Dodwell's Beijing manager, Mr Liu, was charming and helpful. He offered me the use of the guest bedroom suite adjoining their office. So I moved into comparative comfort. There was a picture on the wall of a young Queen Elizabeth.

In the evening Mr Liu took me out for a superb dinner of dishes from all over China: hot and spicy ones from Sichuan, sweet and sour from Hebei, and white fungi soup from Yunnan. All delicious. The Chinese custom I had already noticed is not to talk while you're eating, they usually just concentrate on the food, but Mr Liu has adopted some Western ways and we talked throughout the meal. His quick intelligence made him an enjoyable companion. He expounded the differences between Western and Eastern business manners. Westerners are always in a hurry, speaking bluntly, getting straight to the point. Whereas in China if you want something, you should say you don't like it. When he looks at things from his point of view, he knows what's happening and what to expect, but when he takes the standpoint of a European looking at the Chinese, he doesn't know how to react because he has no way of knowing what 'Chinese' means to us. Mr Liu had never thought of becoming part of a trading company. He had trained as a doctor until the Party sent him to foreign language school. Nor did he begrudge the compulsory five years he spent as a peasant farmer, though his background as a city boy in Beijing must have made life difficult. Now seconded to Dodwell International, married with one child, a son, he is in many ways a model Chinese man of today. I asked him how many children his friends' families have and he replied that most couples are succeeding in only having one child, unless the baby is a girl, in which case, they may accept the penalties of having a second child. As I understood it, there is no actual law about having only one child, but a system of incentives which give the one-child parents a better salary, better housing, greater health care, and preferential treatment for school and job applications. It would be quite persuasive, though I felt sorry for all those only sons when they grow up and find not enough young women to marry. The fact is that China's population is increasing by about twelve million people a year. Already the Chinese comprise a quarter of the world's total population. Modernisation and increased productivity are simply not keeping pace with the increasing number of mouths to be fed. China cannot advance while each week there are a quarter of a million more people than the week before. When I cycled to the Temple of Heaven I watched old people wheeling their grandchildren in the park, in strange bamboo prams built to accommodate several children. But each had one infant in poignantly solitary splendour. Their grandparents strolled with them, singing to them and keeping them amused with the delight of people who love children.

Mr Liu was enthusiastic to help me try to find the house where my grandparents had lived in Beijing. They came to China in 1919 and lived first in Shanghai (where their two sons were born). A few years later they moved to Hankow and then to Beijing, where they lived for seven years before moving on to Tientsin. In those days foreigners in Beijing usually lived in the Legation Quarter. (There were legations – including British, French, American – and each group had its own army guards, for ceremonial purposes.) But my grandparents didn't want to live inside the Legation Quarter, they took a house in the Tartar city.

To find the house would not be easy although my mother had told me the address and location. Even if the quarter had not been demolished long ago, the lane had probably been renamed. Any tall building, and theirs was three storeys, was likely to have fallen in the 1976 earthquake; or been destroyed as bourgeois during the Cultural Revolution. The address was 57, Sui An Pou Hutung, which had been a lane somewhere near the Chi Hua Men Gate in the old Tartar wall. Chi Hua Men Gate and the Tartar wall had now vanished, but Liu said he knew where it had stood because the moat was now a subway. He asked if I minded riding on the back of his small motorbike, and I said that would be fine. Liu proved to be a good driver and we negotiated the traffic, though not without incident. A policeman stopped us for wrongly overtaking a bus (motorbikes aren't allowed to weave through traffic), and he fined us 4 yuan (£1.30), which seemed reasonable. He didn't mind that we weren't wearing helmets, though I thought it was compulsory.

As a cross-reference to the house, my mother had also mentioned Hataman Street, so we went to the end of it nearest the site of Chi Hua Men Gate's site, and cruised around the area but without finding any street called Sui An Pou Hutung. Liu stopped several times to ask for directions, but it was a problem to find anyone who knew the area well. After getting lost we came out at Chien Men Gate, which was where my mother had seen the arrival of the Paris to Peking 1932 Citroën Expedition. My grandmother had interrupted the nursery school-time and bundled the nanny and children into the car, to take them all to wave at the Citroëns as they entered Beijing.

Finally, in a warren of lanes, Liu's bike screeched to a halt and he pointed to a street sign, which I couldn't read because it was in characters. 'Look, look,' he said excitedly, 'the name is not changed, this is Sui An Pou Hutung.' My spirits soared. However, No. 57 was clearly the wrong place – it was a small concrete bungalow. The mystery was solved when a resident said that the numbers had been changed. She didn't know which house had been No. 57, but she sent for an old woman who had lived in this lane all her life. While we waited for her we puttered up and down and found the house ourselves. Being three-storey, there was only one possible candidate and it fitted my mother's description exactly in the way it faced sideways with its front verandah leading on to the garden. Its tall garden wall hid the ground floor from the lane, and the iron gates were locked. So I knocked loudly and repeatedly but no one answered. The house looked empty but not derelict. A passer-by said that it now belongs to the security bureau, but its purpose is unknown.

When the elderly resident arrived we shook hands and she seemed pleased that I'd come here, yet suspicious of me. She said that her family had no particular contact with mine (in those days outsiders were still foreign devils), yet she remembered the children, because the Chinese love children. These were fair-haired toddlers, and one of them (my mother) went very blonde in the sun. The pets they had kept were dogs and a donkey, and stabled elsewhere were four or five racing ponies. The household had been large by British standards, but not by Chinese ones, having a staff of ten Chinese who ran the house. The British nanny didn't count as staff, she was one of the most loved members of the family. To support his establishment my grandfather was a partner in a firm of chartered accountants, with many diverse professional interests; he was highly regarded for his astute mind and incorruptibility.

More elderly residents arrived and I was able to try piecing together the house's history since my grandparents had moved from Beijing to Tientsin (Tianjin-shi Province) in 1932. It had been occupied by a Chinese politician who came to a sticky end soon after the Japanese invaded in 1941. My grandfather came close to a sticky end at the same time in Tientsin; the Japanese tended to annihilate people with influence and dear Grandpa presumably qualified as one. He was put in a Japanese prison, underground, where he was held for seven months. The only thing that he would ever tell me about that period was that one day when he was being taken for interrogation he saw an old man with matted hair coming towards him. The old man's clothes hung off him in rags, and from his tall build he must have once been a commanding figure. My grandfather moved his hand to push back his dark brown hair, and the old man did the same to his white hair, with identical timing. It was his reflection in a mirror.

The rest of his story was something I never tired of listening to in my teenage years whenever he came to stay. He had escaped with a boatload of diplomats and 'censored' people, going by ship to Africa where he spent several years before returning to England. Well before the war, my mother, aged thirteen, had left with the nanny and gone to continue her schooling in England. The fate of the house during the invasion and the Second World War was not known but it had obviously been cared for. During the Cultural Revolution, the local residents said, the Red Guards took away some doors and windows but they didn't wreck the place. After the revolution it became the residence of a famous geologist, Lisu Guang, who lived there until his death, and its next tenant was the deputy director of Beijing Public Security Bureau. In the 1976 earthquake it was damaged but was repaired in the succeeding years. They said that its interior layout had remained the same, but because it is low-profile security, I could not have permission to enter it. So I gazed in from outside, letting my imagination restore latticework flower trellises to its anonymous grey façade. It had been a much-loved home, and it gave me a glow of pleasure to stand there at the door. Locked out, I felt almost as though I'd just forgotten my key.

Stories and memories from two generations crowded into my mind. Grandmother Doris Beddow was quite a lady to follow. Various articles survive from her days as a special correspondent in China. One is an account of events within the besieged city of Hankow and of meeting the Warlord Chang Tso Lin. It was the first time that he'd officially met a European woman. The meeting took place in his palace outside Beijing; Doris remarked on the number of armed sentries and on the silver mail vest that the warlord was wearing for protection against assassins.

At first glance one could not see why the man has attained such power . . . he obviously has no nerves and no humanity, but he is one of the people and his appearance is that of the coolie which he is by birth. I was certainly impressed, but not by the man, merely by the numbers and weapons of his guards.

Doris wasn't a long-distance traveller like Ella Maillart, or the Misses Cable and French, she just wanted to see more of China and her restless spirit drove her into making week-long jaunts into the countryside. She learned to speak Mandarin and, hiring mules, she would go off along trails, taking her camp bed strapped to a mule's back. At night she'd put up her bed in the courtyards of temples and monasteries. She obviously enjoyed her creature comforts. Travelling with plenty of food, she had eggs and bacon for breakfast and mentions a fat abbot who ate her complete jar of jam, 'and when empty he put it down with a sigh of regret'.

In showing her a temple's valuables of jade and porcelain, a monk once produced a prized vase which proved to be an old brandy bottle complete with label. A perfect bronze lotus was set in its mouth. The monk explained that he had drunk Wine of the Gods from the bottle, and deemed that it must continue to hold something rare and equally precious. Doris was unfortunately not equipped to provide a refill. That journey had taken her to a sacred mountain in Shensi Province, visiting on the way the Valley of the Lost Tribe (which I couldn't find), where a group from Beijing had lived in exile for 200 years, and were still wearing hairstyles with a frontal horn-shape made by binding hair with wool.

Doris wasn't over-concerned with social, political or ecological issues; she loved to travel for its own sake, somewhat as I do now. Occasionally she took friends on her jaunts, and when my mother was old enough she took her along too. In summer the two of them, accompanied by a groom, went for long rides on horseback along the coast of the Yellow Sea, and on several occasions my mother recalled meeting smugglers.

They had a huge organised racket going on beyond one of the estuaries, in the early mornings. There were always lots of bundles and baskets coming ashore from the sampans, but I never paid attention to what was in them, and the smugglers didn't usually mind us riding through. And one time your grandmother took us children by car to see the retreat of a warlord's army. They were retreating down the road as we drove along and then we were ordered off the road. It made us very late home, Grandpa was worried frantic, and Doris was so angry about being prevented from driving home that she wrote to the general demanding an apology.
The general's apology duly arrived, bearing so many official

seals that Doris used it as a travel pass on her next journey. People were so awed by the seals that they didn't dare stop her.

I admired her spirit.

Most of us as children have played the game Grandmother's Footsteps, trying to creep up on the 'grandmother' without being seen to move. Now I was in China, I hoped that in some way Doris's spirit could see me as I set out to follow her footsteps on a short journey in a north-westerly direction starting from where the Western Hills rise out of the flat alluvial plain. On the near side of the mountains the paths are well-maintained because the area has become known as a beauty spot and is nowadays within easy reach of Beijing by modern transport. From a village on the lower slopes I began walking up into the hills, on paths that run steeply through pine woods. Birdsong echoed in the valleys and the scent of wild flowers hung in the air. The Western Hills are also called the Fragrant Hills, they were used as hunting-grounds by many emperors.

Doris wrote: 'After loading the three pack mules and a donkey with 250 lbs of provisions and camping equipment we set off up the steep rocky trail . . . the valley narrowed as it ascended, wild flowers flourished, and I picked some walnuts as we passed under a walnut tree.' Later she mentioned reaching a stream which had pools deep enough for diving into, so she stopped to swim. It seemed to me, reading through her journeys, that she stopped to swim every time she found a stream or river. 'In some gorges 500 feet high, I stopped to swim for so long that the mules went on ahead and it wasn't until afternoon that I found them again.' That night she stayed at a temple, sleeping on her camp bed in the courtyard until thunder and lightning drove her to move in among the warrior gods. 'The side gods were decorated with the priests' winter hats. The smell of incense and stored grain made me sleep lightly, and a camel caravan arrived for water during the night.' But it was an improvement on the following night at a temple where she slept sandwiched between two coffins.

The first temple that I saw in the hills was the Temple of Azure Clouds, built as a nunnery in 1331. Nearby was the temple of the Arhats which has five hundred statues of Buddha, carved from wood and covered in thick gold lacquer each representing a different Bodhisattva. From the path I had taken it was not far to another pavilion. To my surprise it was a memorial to Sun Yat-Sen, whose Kuomintang forces ruled China for a brief spell. Sun's ornate sarcophagus, donated by Russia, is still in mint condition. My grandmother had attended his deathbed in 1925, another of her journalistic triumphs, being the only Western woman there in his last moments.

Doris died when I was nine; I only remember her as an old lady in a wheelchair, crippled by arthritis. The photograph albums that I'd browsed through showed her as tall, slim and elegant, with short auburn hair. I couldn't even find the temples and monasteries she had described and, according to the peasants I asked, they had been destroyed. But there were other small temple-monasteries, locked in behind closed doors and high stone walls. The only times I saw into them was from a height, their swept earth courtyards and pillared temples, with curved eaves and shady trees, giving them a peaceful, meditative air.

As I descended, because I had lost her trail, I realised that one doesn't always have to succeed. Success and failure are measuring sticks against others, and I am not interested in that. Let others do their thing. I shall do mine. From afar floated the noise of bus-loads of Chinese day-trippers arriving at the lower temples. The enormous number of people in China means that only the far-flung regions have empty space. It was time for me to start afresh, search out some lesser-known territory and make my own trail there.

12   Into Tibet

The search took me to a remote province bordering Tibet, called Qinghai Autonomous Region. It is also known as 'Inner Tibet', the most sparsely populated province in China, comprising high-altitude ranges, lake basins and swamps. The province used to be completely closed, but within the last year some places in it have opened. To reach Qinghai (Q is pronounced Ch) I travelled by train to Xining, the provincial capital. For the latter part of the journey my companions carried baskets of big healthy cauliflowers, marrows, tomatoes, radishes and boxes of cheeping ducklings.

It's not uncommon to see a man looking after a child in China, the men seem to be much more able than Western men to cope with the messy side of children's needs without any fuss. At mealtimes a man will sit feeding his child with practised ease, and afterwards hold it in his arms until it falls asleep.

The railway goes alongside a river, its muddy reddish colour stands out against the emerald green valleys, and echoes the red earth of landslides in the mountains. As the steam train chuffs uphill, the mountains become redder and their gashed sides are the colour of raw meat. Zigzag paths lead up to the plateauland. My neighbour was a Han biologist who pointed out how the peasants are now growing cash crops of wheat, highland barley, rapeseed and legumes such as broad beans and peas. The fields rolling past were a feast of lushness, making my eyes feel relaxed. Green is so restful to the eyes, especially after being in a smoggy city. As we neared Xining I saw beehives alongside the track, and looked forward to tasting some honey.

After getting my bearings in Xining and obtaining a special permit to be in the area, I set off west hitch-hiking with my canoe for Qinghai Lake, the largest lake in China with an area of 1,630 square miles. But the second truck-driver who gave me a lift said he was going to Lhasa. Why didn't I come too? It would only take five days because the road was good before the rains start. This proposition out of the blue stirred some mixed emotions in me. Of course I longed to go to Tibet, but I had no permit for Lhasa and would certainly be discovered. It seems unnecessary to look for trouble, and I don't really agree with breaking laws; especially if it means possible deportation. I considered a while. The terms of my permit prohibited me from stopping in any towns that were not listed on it. Therefore I deduced that I could go to an area where there is no town, and I asked Wang to drop me at a Tibetan nomad camp anywhere in the mountains before we reached Lhasa.

The drive took three and a half days. From open grassy mountains at about 7,000 feet the road undulated across a vast plateau, then rose to higher flat grassy plains where herds of yaks were grazing, great shaggy beasts, mostly black, others brown, white, or black and white. When we approached in the truck they lowered their horns speculatively then, seeing our size, they turned and bolted away, shaking their large furry heads and waving their long bushy tails. I laughed at their antics, but Wang, the driver, said they can be a nuisance. He was rather dull company because, being Han Chinese, he didn't share my enthusiasm for the Tibetans. He said that they're smelly and dirty people. He also said that Lhasa is being modernised and given a new lease of life. I interpreted his words to mean that the old town is being demolished and replaced with modern concrete buildings. Yet perhaps it's only the tourists who appreciate the quaint old houses; perhaps their occupants are fed up with the leaking roofs and difficult conditions; perhaps they are pleased to be given new houses which are convenient and easy to keep clean, and perhaps to them the concrete buildings are beautiful. None the less, Lhasa sounds a depressing place at the moment and I didn't regret not going there. Besides, it wasn't Lhasa I yearned to see, it was the countryside. I still found it hard to believe that I was on my way to Tibet. It's odd how chance strikes.

We passed through some villages of mud houses and roadside trade stores. Most of the people were brown-skinned Tibetans with felt hats whose broad brims were pulled down at a cowboy angle. At the trading posts the Tibetan horsemen tethered their steeds and unloaded bales of wool from the pack horses. They would trade their wool for supplies of *tsamba* flour. Wang said that they also barter gold, silver and peacock feathers. From far away we heard a resounding clap of thunder but when I looked up thunder in my dictionary Wang said no, not right. In Xinkiang I'd sometimes heard similar thunderous noises on blue sunny days, and had come to the conclusion that they were explosions. There are reputed to be some major testing sites around here. But we saw only the barren undulating plateau and the occasional Tibetan.

Among the more recent travellers in China that I admire is a lady of the Victorian era called Alexandra David-Neel, who walked 2,000 miles from China to Lhasa dressed as a Tibetan pilgrim. She was one of few in those days who managed to reach Lhasa. She spoke Tibetan fluently and lived her disguise so deeply that her passion for Tibet never died. She went on to become a lama in her own right. To some extent the lure of Lhasa was not so much the lure of the unknown as of the forbidden. She believed that no government had the right to interfere with people's natural right to travel where they chose. But in China, permits have always been necessary; it was no different for Marco Polo, who was given the Khan's gold tablet of safe conduct, while a later traveller's passport was an imperial yak's tail. My alien's card is simply a modern tourist equivalent. An inquisitive nature and a zest for knowledge must surely be the hallmarks of all inveterate travellers, and for the other useful attributes I'd suggest a sense of humour in adversity, a calm temper, quick wits, endurance and an ability to sleep in the most obscure and uncomfortable places.

At nightfall Wang kept on driving and I fell asleep wrapped up in my sleeping bag, until I awoke freezing cold to find he had parked for a cat-nap. When I next woke he was driving again. And so it went on for three days, though we stopped one night at a truckers' inn. It was a relief to feel confident that I could travel as an individual without sex hassles. Chinese men don't look at you with that sort of eye. If anything, they see you as a freak. My alien's permit was inspected by some men at the inn, they checked it and gave it back to me.

We went through a couple of fairly large towns but whenever I asked for their names, Wang mentioned places that weren't marked on my map. Wang's lack of conversation was equal to the scenery's lack of mountains. There hardly seemed to be any. It was high, arid plateauland. I had expected jagged peaks and dizzy cliff-hanging roads. We crossed the Kunlun range, which I'd last seen in its western limits near Kashgar. The road didn't seem to be going uphill and it was only from the gradients of streams that I could tell how steeply we were rising. The following day we traversed up to another mountain pass and I guessed that we had reached about 14,500 feet. The altitude made me feel tired so I was content to pass the time by dozing and having slightly inane talks with Wang. The only time I saw him animated was suddenly one day when he jammed on the truck's brakes and, leaving the engine running, he went racing away across the turf. A rabbit dashed ahead of him, dodging in bounds among the tussocks, and Wang followed in hot pursuit. The rabbit vanished into a large tussocky mound and although Wang searched it inch by inch he could find nothing. Two Tibetans turned up and helped him. They all looked slightly silly bending over with their rumps in the air, searching minutely for a rabbit. Needless to say they didn't find it, and Wang returned, taciturn as ever.

Later he reluctantly taught me the few words of Tibetan that he can speak: How are you – *Cho-temo*; thank you – *Qua-dun-chay*; and goodbye – *Ba-day-mor*. But he was sulky about teaching me because he disapproves of anything Tibetan. He wasn't keen to let me leave the truck before Lhasa but when we were about halfway across Tibet, in a region of wide green valleys dotted with Tibetan tents, I insisted on being dropped. Wang still didn't like the idea, and suggested that he would pick me up again on his way back in three days' time. Since it would save me some trouble and since he genuinely seemed to be worried, I agreed to his scheme.

Then we waved goodbye and I went striding across the dry marshland towards some distant tents. These tents, like the Kazakh yurts, are a summer home, but are differently constructed and can be square, rectangular or rounded. Their guyropes of twisted leather held up by poles and pulled tautly angular made me think of long-legged spiders. At first I didn't go close to the ones I passed, they looked closed but I could see fierce Tibetan dogs chained near them. Within half an hour people started arriving back at the camp; they noticed me immediately and I greeted them with a *cho-temo*. Before long one family asked if they could give me shelter for the night. Their tent was a roomy twenty-foot square, with a fire set in a clay trough, and fuelled by animal droppings. The smoke went out through a gap on the leeward wall of the tent, and the windward side was pegged firmly to the ground. A young boy was working a fire bellows made from a dog's skin complete with fur, its legs tied to prevent air escaping. The family's three generations were dominated by an old man in a fur-lined coat. His face had lines of authority and the womenfolk hurried to give him tea.

That night, although the temperature outside was extremely cold, inside was warm and I slept well, sharing quilts with a young unmarried daughter called Paramon. There was a small shrine in the tent, set out with bowls of oil, dried butterfat, some beads and some Buddhist pictures. By day the sleeping area was cleared and the quilts folded in tall piles. Sheepskins were scattered on the floor. In the kitchen area were some sacks of *tsamba* flour, a pile of dry dung, a collection of pots and kettles, and half a sheep which was hanging up to dry.

For breakfast we ate *tsamba* (toasted barley flour), which we stirred into our tea using our fingers, and adding a dollop of yak butter. The children were nimble-fingered and adept at blending together the *tsamba* and butter, squeezing it into round wadges. Mine tasted good but had rather a lot of animal hairs in it. Afterwards the twelve-year-old son went out to saddle his pony and, at my request, he also saddled one for me. The one he gave me was very docile, slightly sluggish, and it was an effort to keep the beast cantering for more than a few paces before it slowed into a triple-jog, though this latter pace was comfortable and he could keep it going for miles.

Our excursion was to round up some yaks and take them to further pastures. I enjoyed the rounding-up, the yaks were easily grouped and our cries of *sssht* got them moving in the right direction. The boy's idea of driving them was at times more like a stampede, galloping his pony around their rear and chivvying them along. Despite the fun my hands went numb with cold because I had no gloves, and the biting cold wind seemed to reach the core of my bones. There had been a light frost in the night, which still coated higher patches of ground. Yet with the effort of urging on my lazy pony I warmed up. The saddle was ill-fitting and wooden – no wonder it was spare. Its stirrup leathers were too short for my legs but they couldn't be altered. My body was beginning to ache when finally we reached a rocky knoll and the boy said that I must turn back. Whether he thought it was too far for me or for my clapped out nag, I don't know, but I did as he asked. With a wave he was gone, shepherding the yaks over the brow, and I turned my pony back across the valley. At an outlying tent an old woman invited me to stop for a cup of tea. Her grandchildren howled with fright at my appearance and hid behind the curtains at the back of the tent. The old woman was fussed by this, and not wanting to cause worry, I didn't stay long.

Passing another tent I nearly got savaged by a Tibetan mastiff; it leapt up at my pony, barking viciously. But it wasn't trying to bite the pony, it wanted to bite me. Fortunately my sober-

minded steed didn't panic, I pulled my legs up high and slapped
his neck to make him hurry away. Later in my three-day stay I
helped Paramon with the annual chore of ear-tagging the family
sheep. Paramon and her mother had sat making the strings
from twisted wool, doubled and knotted. The father had torn
a cloth rag into strips, and I attached the strings to the strips.
To attach these labels of ownership, we first caught and tethered
the sheep, then Paramon stitched the label through the ear.
The sheep struggled like mad and since the rest of the family
had gone about its business I helped her out by trying to hold
the sheep steady. It was quite a battle. Even with the sheep
gripped between my knees, and my hands holding its horns as
handlebars, trying to keep him still, he reared, ducked and
struggled until occasionally we all fell to the ground.

Afterwards we went into the tent for a bowl of milky tea.
Paramon told me that her father owns forty sheep, five horses
and twelve yaks. When any tea-bowl was empty it was immediately refilled, and if a person was hungry he just added some
tsamba. It can be drunk as a thin warming gruel, or thickened
until tacky or solid. Different ingredients can be used including
chunks of natural brown sugar, dried butter fat, wet butterfat
and yoghourt. Most meals consisted of *tsamba*, but I never got
bored with it. It is tasty and satisfying, though I did wish it had
fewer hairs in it.

Milking the yaks was a daily chore for Paramon. Her buckets
are made from wooden slats joined and sealed with a waxy
substance. The calves are tethered overnight so that the cows
have plenty of milk by morning. Paramon squatted down with
her arms lost under the animal's great shaggy belly, and milked
it, leaving enough for the calf. When the calves were untied
they bounded over to their mothers, frolicking and frisking with
high kicks before settling down to drink. Paramon says that
some milk is used for yoghourt and the rest she has to churn
with a wooden club in a tall bucket. I looked in at the bucket's
thick grey scum and wondered how long it has to be churned.
For milk or yoghourt she said that she pounded it for about
two hours, and much longer for butter.

The family's hospitality to me was tremendous and I tried to
repay it with small gifts of flick-lighters and nail-scissors. Part
of the warmth of their home comes from their spontaneous
smiles. It was the same in most of the tents that I visited. The
only problem was the dogs, and people often warned me that
they would attack me so I made sure that I always had a

pocketful of stones, and somone gave me a stick to carry for extra protection. My walks weren't very extensive; within an hour the cold wind numbed my face and feet. The young boy children kept warm by having rough and tumble wrestling matches, rolling on the ground wriggling and laughing. Their daily work was to mind the herds, and sometimes I'd find one of them lying down and singing lustily to himself. The line-ends were shouted with a gusto that echoed across the hills and was lost in the breeze. This really is the roof of the world, and on my walks I could appreciate the lofty air, icy brooks and the silence of wild majestic solitude, in this land which is the nearest place on earth to heaven.

My walks were also the only opportunities I got for washing my face and hands, a custom that my hosts didn't seem to use. I could see why Wang had said that Tibetans are dirty people. The cold is not the only reason why they seldom wash. Some believe that not washing saves them from being turned into fishes after their death, or that spring water contains evil spirits because it comes from inside the earth where the female principle rules. The water only becomes good if exposed to sun and air, part of the male upper world. There's probably a logical reason for this belief. Actually the problem of smell is not so bad in winter when the weather freezes and the rancid butterfat in their clothes helps to keep the people warm.

My most convenient washing place was in an icy brook nearby; it was certainly too cold for a bath but was adequate for a speedy wash. I wondered where the stream went and what other rivers it became part of: the sources of four of the great rivers of the world rise in Tibet: the Yangtse, the Indus, the Brahmaputra and the Mekong.

One afternoon I watched Paramon helping a friend to do her hair. Her previous braids had been unplaited and combed out down nearly to her waist. Starting from the top and dividing the hair into small amounts, Paramon began the coiffeur session. She said that hair needs doing every two weeks, though I think she had no concept of time and probably meant every six months, judging by the untidy state of most women's braids. Her fingers were nimble. As soon as one plait was half done she passed it to her friend who finished it off. The plaits had to be all of the same length, and for those which would be too short the girls added in some long twists of yak wool. They also use red-dyed wool or cord, braiding it in and making patterns out of the way the plaits join. Paramon's twenty plaits were joined at descending levels down her back making a V-shape until only two fat braids remained. They ended together with a silver brooch and a black yak's wool tassel. The most elaborately decorated hairstyle that I'd seen was a cape of plaits evenly attached to a wide strip of embroidered material with all manner of silver chains, medallions, buttons and coral beads. For convenience while working the braids are tucked into the back of the girl's waistband. Someone with a great many usually gathers them together on to a loop of stone or jade.

Jewellery is prized and flaunted, and valuable pieces are inherited by daughters. From women's waist sashes hang silver pendants with coral beads set in them, and some with turquoises. Coral's popularity goes far back. Marco Polo mentions it, observing with Venetian shrewdness that it grew more expensive as it was traded inland, especially in Tibet. From their waist sashes many women suspend a metal double hook which Paramon said is for carrying your pails of yak butter. I asked her if yaks' wool has many purposes and she said that it is so useful that they shear the wool off the yaks and sheep each year. Its primary use is for making the exterior felt of their tents. When I suggested that wool roofs would leak in the rain she said that the hair is naturally waterproof and they do not need to mix any substance with it.

A commotion outside and slight wobbling of the tent sent me scurrying out of the door flap, to where a pony had got tangled in the guy ropes. He wouldn't let me untangle him, being afraid of me – I suppose I smell different from Tibetans – but finally I chased him until he was unwound. The girls hadn't stirred position, they were intent on their work. It seemed a far cry from our idea of going to the hairdresser, with all the preliminary washing and cutting before curling or setting. Paramon couldn't see the point of us Westerners cutting our hair and having to brush it daily. In braids it needs no daily attention. The hairdressing session came to an end. The final touch was an ornate hairclip inherited from her mother's family. Paramon asked if we have this same custom, and I said yes, we did – though all I have inherited has been a little cash and a powerful wanderlust.

On the third day of my stay I packed my rucksack and kept in sight of the road. Wang arrived as he had promised. He still didn't understand why I hadn't wanted to see Lhasa.

13 The biggest lake in China

The mighty Qinghai Lake was created by a vengeful Tibetan god who had been disobeyed by his people. So he tried to drown them. Water burst out of a great hole in the earth, flooding the land until they begged for forgiveness. The god repented and sent an eagle carrying a rock, which it dropped to plug the hole. The rock is the big island in the lake.

I was in my canoe paddling toward the western end of the lake, back on the course I had proposed for myself before being persuaded over the Tibetan border by Wang. According to Ella Maillart, who was here in 1935 with Peter Fleming, the waters of Qinghai Lake are sacred and no boat had ever tried to navigate on it. On a headland at the western end there is a nesting ground for wild geese and gulls. The birds sat in flocks on the ground and only moved away when I walked across. It was amazing the number of nests scattered underfoot and almost invisibly camouflaged. I picked my way carefully. The speckled eggs were well hidden too. And as I stared at the nests around me I became aware that hatching was in process. Eggs were beginning to crack open, a gosling's beak poked out of one, soon followed by his head. Then he paused for a moment to look around; while beside his egg another cracked wide, a golden downy gosling stepped out and sat down in the sun to dry his wet fluff. Cheeping noises began to fill the air. It was a strangely wonderful experience. Some of the parent birds were brave enough to ignore me and return to their nests. Others began to get upset; they wheeled in circles, rending the air with screeching, cawing and honking noises.

A little further along the lakeshore there were cliffs where black cormorants nested. To the Chinese the cormorant symbolises unique ability: to fly, swim, dive and swim underwater. It would be fun to be that adaptable. Apart from that promontory, the lake shore tended to be flat and muddy. Behind it the empty level sands stretched bleak and windswept, until in the far distance they rose up into ice-capped mountains. The northern shore of the lake seemed just as bare, and although I paddled vigorously I couldn't keep warm. (The altitude here is about 10,000 ft.) When I got thirsty I drank some lake water and was

puzzled at its taste. I had forgotten that the lake is salt water,
and undrinkable. This water wasn't a grave problem because
my flask was nearly full and later I saw fresh water coming in
beside some sand dunes. The pools were vividly blue, and gave
rise to tufts of greenery which were being consumed by herds
of yaks and sheep. At least they didn't eat the flowers; the
ground was sprinkled with dwarf iris and tiny blue flowers.
The sand dunes had clumps of thorny brush in purple bloom.
And above it all an eagle floated on the wind. Its wingspan
must have been between six and eight feet. Its shadow rippled
slowly over the dunes. There were no trees. If I wanted to camp
the night by the lake I'd have a problem with lack of firewood.
Local people use dry dung, so I collected some and stashed it
in the canoe before paddling away.

A cold wind blew up, pushing my canoe away from the shore
and, although I steered hard, the wind had the upper hand. It
brought black clouds scudding low over the horizon. I tried to
use the wind at an angle and paddle quickly across to the other
side of the lake. But before we were halfway the rain arrived,
sleeting down. I was already wearing my anorak (and everything else) against the cold, and I pulled the hood over my face.
The animal dung I'd collected got wet and made a mess of the
canoe floor, leaving me sitting in a brown puddle of liquid
dung. Somehow it didn't make me want to laugh. It was a
pretty miserable person who finally reached the beach and
packed up her canoe with hands that were painfully numb.
One of the paddles wouldn't unscrew from its shaft; knowing
that my cold hands were useless I put it like that into my
rucksack; the shaft fortunately divides in two so it only stuck
out a little and looked mildly peculiar. Noticing a Tibetan
woman herding two laden yaks, I hurried over to ask her where
I could spend the night. But she ran away from me, chasing
her yaks along in front of her. Their bundles, jerrycans and
baskets flapped and bounced. My paddle bobbed in pursuit.
But she didn't slacken her pace until I'd given up and she was
far away. So I walked to the road and eventually got a lift in a
minibus carrying a group of Hong Kong tourists to spend a
night at a Tibetan tented camp near the western end of the lake.
They said that if I chipped in with their expenses I would be
welcome to join their tour. I agreed, mainly because I didn't
want to get out again into the rain.

At the camp we were installed in a large and luxurious
colourful tent, specially made for tourists. Silky hangings are

all very well, but not like yak wool when it comes to keeping out the rain. Water leaked in on to the bedding. Outside, in a lull between storms, a sheep was butchered for our supper. I always find freshly slaughtered meat to be tough, and this time was no exception.

Next morning I went for a walk. I came to a shrine, and newly erected prayer flag, set up here to honour the animist spirits which look after the summer grasslands. The ground beneath my feet was a mass of tiny purple orchids. The plain was dotted with sturdy animal pens made from sods of turf, and some mud compounds. Animals must be penned at night because of wolves. The tents here are dramatically black and white. Many of their occupants invited me in to drink tea. In one tent I talked to an elderly woman who had more yak wool than ordinary hair in her braids; her grandchildren sat on a rug and waved some sheep's ribs at us. The family shrine was decorated with bowls, buddhas and a pair of sheep's horns.

When I showed my postcards the old lady was entranced by the picture of Queen Elizabeth in her regal finery. The old lady touched the picture to her forehead and bowed down with reverence. Before leaving I gave her the picture and watched her put it in a place of honour in the shrine.

I'd kept some morsels of yak butter from the old lady to smear around the screw of my jammed paddle. I melted it to run down inside and rather to my surprise, it worked. The blade came sliding off, and the connector was undamaged.

In the afternoon the minibus party made ready to leave. We were only going to drive as far as the eastern end of the lake and stop overnight in a village there. But the drive was made slow because my Hong Kong companions kept wanting to stop and take photographs of sheep, an animal they had never seen before, and not content with mere photography they began to chase them across the plain. But it was harmless fun and they certainly enjoyed themselves. When they grew tired of chasing sheep they sat back in the bus and sang songs in Cantonese and English. Each person in turn was persuaded to sing a song, and not even I was allowed to maintain my inbred barrier of reserve. Their manners toward me were so friendly and polite that I couldn't refuse. I gave them a quick burst of Engelbert Humperdinck's 'Please release me, let me go'.

In the morning the tour guide proudly took us to see the latest thing in mechanical sheep-shearing. I watched the two shearers at work for a few minutes, puzzling as to what kind of Tibetan throwbacks they could be. Their well-tanned skin was only slightly lighter than the rest. But the skill and speed of their work set them apart, and I began to suspect they must be Australians, until one of them stepped back to let a Tibetan take over and I discovered that they were home lads from the north of England. One of them, John, explained how the Tibetans traditionally work by laying the sheep down and working from the top. A more efficient way is to hold the sheep upside down between your knees so that it cannot wriggle. Their previous machinery was poorly sharpened and clumsy to use; it left a lot of wool still on the sheep.

The Englishmen were spending three weeks giving instruction with the new stuff, and although they could not speak Tibetan they were adept at sign language. Just as well, because the machine instruction manuals were written in Chinese, which neither the Englishmen nor the Tibetans could read. But the major complication was that only one machine had arrived, the rest were delayed somewhere en route through China, and if they arrived too late the Englishmen would have to leave without installing them. They were frustrated and depressed about it. The problems of doing business in developing countries always seem greater than one would expect.

My Hong Kong friends were thrilled by the sight of so many sheep, and the lambs, and they sang all the way home in the bus. Our destination was Xining, which suited me because it was where I had left the bulk of my luggage.

14   Taer'si pilgrimage

One reason why I hadn't minded missing Lhasa was because I knew that the most important lamasery in Qinghai had recently been opened to visitors. It was by coincidence that I heard about it, since I'd been trying to trace a lamasery called Kumbum which is mentioned in several old accounts as having been a seat of wisdom and learning. It ranked third among Tibet's most sacred monasteries and once housed more than 3,000 monks in an isolated place, remote from any modern travel routes. Whenever I asked at public security offices people shook their heads about Kumbum and said that they didn't know where it was. After pulling out my photocopies of old maps I eventually located Kumbum not far from Xining. I discovered it is still a functioning lamasery, now called Taer'si and it had been opened in the last three months. I felt that the tracks were finally coming together. Local buses go to Taer'si from Xining every hour, leaving when full. The one I boarded was almost full and among the passengers were several Tibetan Buddhist pilgrims.

At Taer'si I stayed in a hotel close to the lamasery. On the door of my room was pinned the notice 'Foreigner Friends Welcome'. Suddenly I felt exhausted, lay down and slept for the rest of the day. Awakening at 6 p.m. I went out to buy supper, but found that the whole town seems to keep monastery hours; supper hour is 5 p.m. and after that the restaurants and food stalls are closed for the night. Fortunately I found one that was running late and they gave me a dish of chow mein.

The following morning I was up shortly before dawn, in time to watch the lamasery coming to life. As I wandered through the lanes between temples I was passed by a group of monks wearing full-length brown robes, wrapped around their chest and over one shoulder. A couple of them wore thick capes of red and brown wool against the cold. Their heads were shaved bald, though on some the hair was growing back in a light crew-cut. Their morning starts with a formal meditation period. An insistent drumbeat could be heard, growing faster and more rhythmical. In the centre of the temples stands the Grand Hall of the Golden Roof, whose gold-plated bronze roof is supported

by marble walls. I didn't try to find a way into the Hall, being
content to listen and watch the rays of sun stealing over the
lamasery's red-tiled roofs. Mist was rising slowly from the valley
below, the drumbeat continued, and I could smell fresh bread
being baked somewhere nearby. When the first rays of sun
touch the temple doorsill, the formal meditation period ends.

Outside on the Holy Road, sannyasis (novice monks) hurried
to the wells with water buckets slung on their shoulder yokes.
Most carriers were humming and singing to themselves, and
the birds set up a riotous dawn chorus. The early pilgrims on
the Holy Road were mostly Tibetan families, men in black velvet
coats lined with lambswool; women in long padded coats of
red and black, tied around the waist with rather grubby sashes
from which hung an assortment of silver pendants. Their hair,
in the customary plaits, was caught together at the back with
silver loops and embroidery. I followed a pilgrim family into a
temple since they seemed to know which doors to go through.
The entrances are flanked by bronze dishes of butterfat and the
stone lions and statues are smeared in fat by pilgrims to show
their respect. Several temple-shrines containing Buddha statues
are surrounded by prayer wheels, large, upright barrels painted
with gold characters on red, or beaten bronze; each wheel
creaks on its axis as the pilgrims walk around the shrines setting
the barrels slowly spinning. Prayer wheels can be any size, and
some individual ones are so large and sacred that pavilions
have been built to house them. On entering these shrines the
pilgrims each grasp one of the prayer wheel's wooden handles,
drop their written prayer paper in the tray beneath the wheel,
and walk around once while pushing the wheel before emerging
back into the sunshine. The turning of the wheel is meant to
activate their prayers, and as they revolve the big wheels make
noises like the clashing of cymbals and the thunder of horse's
hooves on a baked plain. From there I tracked the pilgrim family
to the Main Hall of Meditation; outside it was a line of old
leather boots; devotees must pray barefoot.

Inside the vast hall are pillars, silken banners, prayer flags,
tapestries, thousands of Buddha pictures, and at one end three
seated statues. The pilgrims prostrated themselves, touching
their foreheads to the floor, three times in front of each statue.
The wooden flooring in front of each has been worn into dips
where countless faithful pilgrims have made obeisance here
over the centuries.

One of the statues was of Tsong Khapa, the fourteenth-century founder of the Tibetan Buddhist Yellow Hat sect. The lamasery is built over his birthplace. Legend says a tree grew on the spot and the fragrance of its leaves could be smelt five miles away. In the same temple compound there are statues of former Dalai Lamas and the third Dalai Lama's remains. Stepping into a separate walled courtyard, I found a shady green and flowery temple garden, the lilac bushes were in bloom and their scent was like summer wine. In the main hall of the oldest temple compound is a thirty-foot-high pagoda under which Tsong Khapa is said to be buried amid precious objects and lamps of gold, silver and bronze. Along the walls are libraries of scriptures in Tibetan and Mongolian. At the back of that temple I watched a priest painting a new screen. He used powder colour, dribbling it in thin lines out of a two-foot long hollow pipe, and scratching a ratchet at the top to make the powder spill out evenly. His artist's palette of colours was set out in a multitude of old dishes, probably Ming pottery, and the effect of his artwork was a superb mandala. He said that its purpose is to draw your thoughts in through the shape and colour and to rest your mind on it.

A winding cobbled path up a hillside came out at a temple whose door handles were embellished with streamers and tufts of yaks' wool. Inside that temple is a sculpted pageant of warriors going to battle, people being carried in sedan chairs, attendants, and mountain scenery, but it was rather garish and looked plastic. It wasn't until I realised that the whole thing had been sculpted from butterfat that I appreciated its merit. While I rested on the hillside and listened to wind chimes tinkling, my attention was caught by a sannyasi of about eight years old, firing a catapult down on to passing monks. As ammunition he used hard berries, but his aim was not accurate enough to hit anyone.

By then I was beginning to feel hungry so headed for the Holy Road. Pilgrims now flocked along the road, and in the warm sun they had all pushed their coats back off one shoulder. Apart from the fine-boned Tibetans I noticed groups of fuller-faced Mongols who come from Tsaidam. The pilgrimage, bringing gifts, is believed to assure them of places in heaven. Other pilgrims come in search of understanding, or to do penance and gain forgiveness for sins, or to make vows and to give thanks. Ahead of me was a blind woman being led along by the hand by a five-year-old boy. The road down the hill from the lamasery is flanked by local restaurants, and trade stores

and stalls selling beads for the Tibetans to use in their jewellery.
Coral and amber, and some stones from far away places: mala-
chite, tiger's eye and moonstones. Necklaces and hats were
being tried on by one family, and a store keeper explained to
me that while the Tibetans buy jewellery the Mongolians tend
to buy long-stemmed tobacco pipes, tobacco pots, and small
jars of polished stone. And tourists buy more than either group.
It was tempting to stop and browse but I remembered my
hunger and feared that if I was late for lunch the cafés would
close again.

Looking in to see what was cooking I settled for some noodles
and mutton. After I'd bought a bowl of tea the woman hurried
over and dumped a handful of nut shells into it, then added a
scoop of clear stuff that looked vaguely like ice but turned out
to be honey. Delicious, a Hui custom, this must be a Hui
restaurant. On the walls I noticed posters of Hui generals on
horseback, and was struck by the thought that each general
had the same expression on his face as his horse. Well, we say
that people grow to look like their pets.

There was one temple that I specifically wanted to see and
after a lazy last cup of tea I went back uphill to the monastery
square. Using a sketch-map which someone had drawn for me,
I found my way to this lesser temple. Its mural panels show
old women wearing necklaces of skulls. The women's breasts
hang down to their waists and their faces have expressions
like demons. Another panel is of an active human skeleton
brandishing parts of a dismembered man. Another shows a
washing line of drying human skins, some complete with heads;
others portray people being skinned. It was all a bit gruesome.
On the balcony with their heads overlooking the temple yard
are the real stuffed skins of a bear, bison and antelope, their
horns decorated with coloured cloth streamers. But the animals
are not well stuffed and their shapes are distorted. And around
their eyes the skin is pulled back which gives them a demented
stare. Incense towers were smoking. Small birds were pulling
out scraps of wool and red cloth to take for their nests. A monk
and a boy began to make music with a drum and cymbals,
while the boy chanted words from pages that were wooden
slates.

As I walked back through the monastery and came to the
grassy dell in the loop of the Holy Road, I saw that something
was happening. Young men dressed as warriors were fighting
in pairs. Some had swords whose long metal blades flashed

through the air in mock battle. A solo fighter ran into their centre and leapt into the air, slapping his boots behind his back, and landing in a fighting stance. He followed this with a somersault that flipped him back upright in an attacking move of hands chopping out karate-style. Then everyone stopped to discuss something, standing around and illustrating their words with wild arm movements. A couple of fighters came over to where I sat watching on the bank. They said that they are part of an amateur theatrical troupe, which was rehearsing its routine for a forthcoming performance. The play was about Taer'si lamasery and its history.

The lamasery's evening gathering was at 5 p.m. but I missed it because I had gone for a walk out in the hills. After about two miles I reached a lake and climbed up on to the hill overlooking it. It was peaceful and the hill was carpeted with celandine, cyclamen-coloured ground orchids and golden moss, and miniature blue forget-me-nots. Also thistles and an innocuous-looking plant that stung me when I sat on it. A few minutes later two young girls crept up behind me and sat nearby. One of them sang in Chinese, a soft melodious song. It seemed to round off a satisfying day; the sannyasi evening meeting could be a treat for tomorrow.

That short walk gave me a taste for a longer one and accordingly I set out the next day from behind the lamasery, taking a path which had no signs saying 'Closed to Foreigners'. For a while I walked in the company of a dark-skinned man who twirled a handheld prayer wheel. It was a hot sunny day. From the bald hilltops there were clear views across valleys and villages to distant craggy ranges. On one hilltop was a tall prayer flag, a banner hanging downwards with many small flags attached. Keeping to the ridges I bypassed the villages but could see down into the square-walled compounds, the gardens and trees, donkeys and yaks. For several miles the path led through open fields where people wearing big straw sunhats were weeding their crops. The rolling valleys were a patchwork of green wheatfields, yellow plots of rapeseed, and brown earth being harrowed by single-blade ploughs. At noon when I rested beside a field a family brought a bowl of noodles and potato chunks over to me, and gave me two twigs to use as chopsticks. I demurred at eating their lunch but they showed me that they'd brought a cauldron of it, and a flask of tea in wicker wrapping. Yet their feet were bare and their clothes were so patched that there was more patched cloth than original. The husband began filling his long-stemmed tobacco pipe so I gave him some of my tobacco which he accepted with relish.

They were a happy and relaxed couple, they said that life nowadays is much better than it used to be. The community is doing well and everyone gets enough to eat. Their children go to school, and when they're sick they can get basic medical attention which, although not expert, is much better than nothing. Having markets for excess crops means they can obtain things which before were not easily available. And now that college graduates and townies are no longer ruralised (sent to till fields) the locals don't have to worry about useless inept workers who eat more than they grow! Nowadays there's little to complain about.

Dark clouds scudded over the horizon and while the peasants went back to work I hurried back towards Taer'si. My haste was due both to the storm looming behind me and to the fact that I didn't want to miss the sannyasis' evening meeting. The storm clouds veered away to the north and I arrived back with time to spare. While walking slowly through a temple yard I noticed a middle-aged monk getting ready for the prayer session, doing abasements but like Western men do pressups: I counted 21, 22, 23, from kneeling to flat out with forehead on the floor each time, 36, 37, and on up to 40. Other monks have kneeling pads and they use felt hand pads so their palms will slide easily on the wooden floor.

At the appointed hour I went to the main temple's courtyard and sat with a couple of other tourists in an out-of-the-way nook. On the flagstones sat some lines of young sannyasis, a mixture of children and teenagers from ten to sixteen years old. An equal number of sannyasis stood and hurled questions for them to answer spontaneously. The hurling of questions was accompanied by handclaps and flicking of brown prayer beads, and frequently the boys paced up and down deep in thought. Some questions are about the scriptures and some are philosophical. Spontaneous and sudden enlightenment is sought through intuitive understanding. In general, Buddha didn't teach people to have faith, he taught doubt and questioning. Such doubts may lead one to look into the problem and to gain knowledge, and this was Buddha's intention. The role of teachers is to make their pupils think, doubt and seek. The only truth of any value is the truth that you discover for yourself.

It was a glittering scene; the red and gold prayer wheels surrounding the temples, green and gold roofs, carved pillars, marble and incense; doors of wood decorated with metal scroll-work, guarded by stone lions whose heads gleamed greasily with butterfat offerings. There were about two hundred and fifty monks in residence. It used to be the custom for each family to send one son to the monastery, as much as a method of population control as out of piety. The majority of novice monks in the courtyard were teenagers of about fifteen years old, but there were a few ten-year-olds. A separate group of twenty-year-olds was having a lively discussion about the murals on the yard's inner wall. The atmosphere was high-spirited and it caused some fooling around, which was tolerated by their elders who sat on the temple portico.

In the centre of the elder monks sat an old abbot who was talking animatedly to a man standing in front of him, who in turn talked and waved his hat in the air. About twenty other monks sat listening, their headgear was unusual helmet-type hats crested with wool, looking like exaggerated cock's combs. This is the yellow hat which gives the sect its name. No one sat in the throne chair behind the group. Suddenly they all stood up, put on their cloaks, sat in front of the throne and began to chant in sonorous voices. Taking off their hats one by one more of them joined in, and the old abbot took his seat on the throne. One voice chanted a solo prayer and the rest took up the chorus. Some Tibetan pilgrims kneeling to one side of the courtyard joined in with them. Different people sang different chants and the whole blended together into a round of pulsating sounds. With these sounds they were led into their evening meditation period.

At the end I came away uplifted. Of course I had again missed the town dinner-hour but found the Hui café still open. While waiting for the noodles to cook I worked out my journey ahead, down through western China towards its south-west corner. When I left the Hui couple taught me the words of formal leave-taking, which I translated as, 'I leave the warmth of your presence with sorrow.' To which they replied, 'May happiness and a good road be your fortune.'

15   Tea shops in Chengdu

'But you're going the wrong way around,' the other travellers kept telling me. Everyone starts from Hong Kong and comes up clockwise round the south-west, heading either for the north or for Shanghai or Beijing. I didn't mind going against the flow. It had been good enough for Marco Polo, and it had various advantages such as discovering where to stay on the grapevine, and swapping maps of places I'd been for places that I was going to. Also it meant that I crossed paths with many other travellers instead of being stuck with a bunch who were going at the same speed.

China's furthest south-western province is Yunnan. To reach it I began by taking a train from Xining to Chengdu in Sichuan province, which takes twenty-six hours. Because I hadn't booked in advance there was little chance of getting a sleeper berth, but the train wasn't crowded and after Lanzhou I found an empty row of hard seats to stretch out on.

Question time. In China it's not easy to get information; you have to keep asking questions. People don't volunteer information and even though they may know something that would be useful to you, they will not tell you unless you ask the appropriate question. For instance, they tell you where the daily bus stops but do not tell you that it's already gone. It's made me learn to keep questioning, and re-phrasing my questions until the full answer comes up. The idea lingers that it can be dangerous to give away information; people fear that they may say something which could be used against them, or to discredit China. It used to be forbidden to teach Chinese to foreigners; xenophobia dies hard. In return, people ask me predictable questions. What is my nationality? What is my *ganbu* (work unit), or my job? Usually I say I'm a geography student, or a tourist. How much did my watch cost? Actually it cost £2 in Hong Kong, but cheap Hong Kong watches are not available in China. Am I married with children? Where are my companions? On hearing that I'm alone they say they wouldn't dare do it, and I reply that there's nothing to fear.

How old am I? This question is asked more often than any other, and I've now realised that it's not really because they're curious about my age, it's because my age will tell them how much respect I am due. Age brings seniority. And whenever I don't understand their regional accents I just give them the answers in any order, and watch them laugh because I've given them the information they wanted but none of it matched their questions.

During the last few hours of the train ride to Chengdu it became more noticeable that we were going south. Water-buffalo wallowed in mud-puddles beneath a rainy sky. It had never occurred to me that summer might be the rainiest time of year in China. The countryside was a green kaleidoscope. The train's loud-speakers were never silent. The blaring of loud-speakers is something one learns not to hear; it's such a continual jabber-jabber that I hardly ever notice whether they're turned on or off. Most towns and villages also seem to have loud-speaker systems, they're pervasive: Chinese voices relaying morning physical jerks, telling you that crop production has increased in neighbouring provinces, encouraging people to greater effort, praising good workers, broadcasting political speeches, and requesting people to give up spitting. That's a loser. Spitting is as natural to the Chinese as blowing our noses is to us. They believe the phlegm must be expelled from the body.

The hotel in Chengdu had soft beds and ample hot water every evening, and the city was small enough to be fun by bicycle. In the old part of town the buildings lean against each other, the upper walls are whitewashed between their dark beams; their upper storey leans outward with a balcony and overhanging roof, supported by wooden angles. Some houses have intricately carved wooden supports, latticework and Chinese lions. Balconies seem tacked on to houses as rickety bamboo afterthoughts. People sat outside their street doors in bamboo and wicker chairs, and invited their neighbours to play a board-game similar to draughts. Bean stalks and vines grew up from tubs of earth towards upper storeys and mingled with the pots of flowers hanging from the balconies. Cats prowled around, and song birds trilled from their cages.

Among the residential streets are busy shopping streets selling clothes, stationery, bed springs, food and fruit, and furriers selling animal skins from the mountains – fox, bear, and something that looked like leopard. The sheepskin jackets, vests and overcoats were offered in short wool or long ringlets. Also I stopped at the Blind People's Massage Parlour for a half-hour massage of my tired, aching muscles. Blind people are trained

here as masseurs, a job that they do with ease because blindness
gives them a more finely tuned sense of touch.

Back on my bicycle I joined the traffic. The jingling of bike-
bells filled my ears, and the protesting quacks of ten ducks
strung upsidedown from one bike's handlebars. Bicycles are so
plentiful that at crossroads there are traffic controllers who
shout at you, and blow whistles if you ignore them. They direct
the cyclists with little red flags and a green plastic loud-hailer.
Bicycle loads can be outrageous – when I told someone that I'd
seen a 3-seat sofa on the back of a bike, he capped my story by
saying that he'd seen a bike carrying a full-size sofa with a
passenger sitting on top of it.

In the northern part of town I found a street full of barrows
selling incense and candles and behind them was the entrance to
the Wenshu Monastery. The gateway was flanked by guardian
statues, blue-faced and violent, black-faced and angry, pink-
faced and calmly playing a lute. I guessed that a local festival
was being celebrated because the altars were laden with dishes
of oranges and apples, and flower petals. In the main temple
are many golden Buddhas and Ming vases of gladioli. The
prayer flags and floor cushions reminded me of Taer'si, but the
pilgrims here were from other ethnic minority groups. They
had adopted Chinese clothing, and their faces were shaded by
conical straw hats set on a canework frame which holds the hat
a few inches above the head and allows for circulation of air. A
clever idea, I thought, since the day was hot and muggy. Other
people resting on benches in the courtyard fanned themselves
with red Chinese paper fans, or woven straw ones. Pilgrims
moved to and fro, pausing to genuflect and prostrate themselves, and lighting as many as ten joss sticks at each shrine.

But, for me, the essence of Chengdu was in the tea shops.
Roadside bamboo armchairs and strong leaf-tea. I suppose you
could say they've got it down to an art. The English pride
themselves on tea, having imported it since 1650, when it sold
at £6–£10 per pound, and China tea clippers like the *Cutty Sark*
raced to land the new season's tea in the London docks. When
the House of Dodwell was shipping tea, one of its clippers, the
Stirling Castle, set a record time of forty-five days from Hankow.
But on her return via Singapore the captain was rebuked in
court for having forced the Singapore pilot to jump overboard,
rather than stopping to let him embark on to the pilot boat.

My teapot got knocked over by someone chasing chickens
away from the café, but there was no damage and another pot

arrived, so I rested a moment longer. Dodwell had also sold tea to Russia, compressed bricks of tea, transported by camel caravan which took months. When it became possible for rail transport to be used, there were immediate complaints about the flavour. It transpired that when sent by camel and packed in hessian bags, the tea absorbed some of the camel sweat which contributed to its distinctive flavour. By the Russians, the camel-free flavour was found inferior. So later consignments were packed with camel-hairs in the wrapping. Tea was press-packed into bricks for convenience; I remembered finding one with an ornate design in the attic at home, which my mother had brought back in her school trunk.

16   The stone forest at Shilin

The mountain scenery along this route is justly famous, but sequences of short tunnels leave the eyes confused, flickering between daylight and darkness, while in the longer tunnels sooty smoke pours in through the open windows. When you are on a train you often wish you could be leaping off at some tempting spot. But when we passed the sacred mountain, Emei Shan, I was glad I hadn't stopped. The idea of climbing a mountain with a flight of steps up it, along with hordes of other tourists, in the rain, didn't appeal to me, while the logs floating down to the Dadu river sawmills convinced me I wouldn't have wanted to risk my canoe among them either.

Occasionally I spotted soldiers with rifles on bridge parapets and strategic view points, guarding the hills against the chance of people straying that way. It's an area said to hold top-secret missile-testing bases. On a mountainous stretch my attention was caught by some billowing white smoke which seemed to be escaping from the ground, coming in lines from fissures and cracks in the rock. It couldn't be hot springs because the smoke was coming from the sides and tops of the hills. And every mile there was another armed sentry.

The villagers who live around this railway track are Yi people. Easy to distinguish from the Han Chinese, the Yi women wear robes and turbans as headdresses. The headdress is a sort of bonnet held in place by a fat plait of hair coiled around the head. Some girls had short plaits decorated with silver medallions and big silver bauble earrings. Many Yi women had long-fringed black shawls, others wore blue tunics tied with a sash.

At one station yard a group of six women was scrambling to climb into an empty freight wagon. They had to clamber up the tall sides, pulling and pushing each other; their shawls and laden back-baskets made the climb a difficult task, but doubtless worthwhile if it meant a free ride home. When all six were safely in the wagon they stood peering out over the top, watching what was going on in our train.

The main reason why I was travelling to Kunming and Yunnan was because south-western China has many different minority groups; Yunnan alone has twenty-two, ranging from the Wa headhunters whose village lanes used to be edged with human skulls on posts, to more sophisticated tribes who kept slaves and had feudal systems until the 1950s. Yunnan province is a mountainous tableland that reaches up in steps from the south and west bordering Tibet. It also has borders with Vietnam, Laos, Burma and India. It's called the 'land of perpetual spring'. I wished it would stop raining. Another minority group is a band of Mongols who settled to the south of Kunming after the Mongol Khan's armies had overrun the area. Marco Polo arrived in Kunming a few years later (about 1275); he mentioned animists and nature-worshippers, and people who excelled in magic and mystical arts. One of his reasons for visiting Yunnan was to look for the Elixir of Life. While we in Europe were busy trying to turn base metal into gold, the Chinese were searching for the secrets of immortality. There were two known types of elixir; for immortality or merely for prolonging life. The ingredients were sulphur and quicksilver, but the secret was their exact ratio, and many rulers (including one of the Khans) died from drinking a harmful combination. When Marco Polo reached Kunming he finished writing up his findings and rested in the town's peace and comfort.

Kunming is subtropical, its flower gardens abound with exotic plants, but it's not a really pretty town because of extensive concrete modernisation and bicycle travel is as hectic as everywhere else in China. In one street market I came to the dental section where the displays of teeth in jars, plastercast samples, and foot-operated dental drills awaited customers. No chairs, patients have to stand. It made me glad that my teeth are healthy. Families from various minority groups were in town. Instead of Chinese Mao clothes the women wear side-fastening waistcoats over pale shirts and blue aprons, with blue baggy trousers. The unmarried girls wore red headdresses with pom-poms. A few steps after I'd passed one group I turned around for a second look, at the same moment as the girls turned to stare at me.

Later as I walked along between a canal and a row of old whitewashed houses, admiring their green tiled roofs and wooden façades, I stopped to rest by an archway on to the waterfront. Stone steps led down to stone platforms at water level, where women squatted to wash their clothes and clean their vegetables in the same water. The occupants of a house nearby regarded me with curiosity from the dimness behind their half-opened door, and a pony tethered outside standing between the shafts of a cart dozed and sighed with boredom. Gentle drizzle began falling from the grey sky, so taking out my umbrella I pressed the button to make it open. Unfortunately it had rather a strong spring and as it sprang open it tore from its handle and shot out across the walkway. The pony jerked his head up so violently that his tether broke and, in a panic, he galloped off along the canal walk, with the cart swinging crazily behind him. I felt a strong desire to laugh but, knowing that an accident could happen and feeling responsible, I set off in pursuit. A youth walking ahead heard the pony cart clattering out of control and he waved his arms in front of it, forcing it to skid to a halt. He also helped me to return the pony and cart to its tether, and to assure the owners that no harm had been done.

The youth, whose name was Lin, had been on his way to Wushu practice and, as we walked back towards the town centre, he explained that Wushu is an ancient Chinese martial art. His face lit up as he decribed it, 'You can do Wushu alone, or in twos, or many people. The rules are that you can hit with your heel, knee, leg, arm or head but not using your fist. Keep fighting until you can't fight any more. I practise Wushu every day, it brings me alive but some of the movements are difficult to make accurately and I do not often win the fight.' Later that day I had the chance to watch some Wushu competitions. With their arms swinging innocently, the first pair of fighters approached each other and suddenly one spun his body and jumped, jabbing his foot into the other's stomach. His opponent rolled quickly over backwards and sprang back on to his feet, at the same instant as the first boy jumped and rammed his shoulder into the other's chest. Another belly-kick followed. It had a complex arrangement of steps, and the rapid muscular control looked hard to achieve.

I asked Lin if other martial arts are popular too and he said that violent sports are not encouraged in China. At school you do not play aggressive games, violence isn't admired. Kung Fu is the rage among Hong Kong Chinese, not among the Chinese in China. Here they prefer harmonious types of exercise such as Tai chi chuan. In some ways even the Wushu display seemed more like ballet than fighting.

That evening I went in search of a theatre I'd heard about. It was in an area of dubiously dark alleys. I had a bicycle but no lights. After a half hour ride and stopping to ask several people, who were all helpful, I arrived at a long tin shack. Loud voices and clashes of cymbals echoed out of it and as I went in I paid an entrance fee of four fen. The whole audience turned to stare at me. They were a mixture of minority groups in traditional embroidery as well as Han Chinese. They wouldn't let me slide unobtrusively on to a back bench, but insisted that I took a seat near the front. A family made space for me and the man behind me whispered, 'I can speak a little English and can tell you what is happening.' Thus I came to see a Chinese opera.

The actors were a man in black robes and scraggy long wig, waving a silver wand, an emperor or god who sat on a throne, and an old peasant who sang a propaganda song about the terrible conditions in which people had lived before communism. He sang it to the music of two wooden boards being clapped together. The make-up department had used heavy rouge to give the actors red-shadowed eyes. The musicians looked a little out of place in their army uniforms, but one group struck up a tune with a gong, drum and a lute, while on the opposite side of the stage four violinists played violins varying from a wooden cup on a short post to some longer ones with cylinder bodies.

The plot of the play began to unfold as the scene changed to a family of peasants with two sons. The younger married son was diligent and honest, while the elder son was a lazy foolish man married to a scheming scarlet-faced woman. The actors talked and sang, their speech was punctuated by music, a single stroke of the gong to emphasise a point, or the cry of a violin. One musician's violin stem broke from its base but the man simply melted some wax into the join to cement it. The actors strutted around using exaggerated postures, and guffaws of laughter came from the audience as the scheming wife spat back at her relatives who confronted her with home truths; the diligent wife worked thread while she talked; and although the singing of all the actors was a bit raucous and not tuneful, it was full of meaning and inflections. Suddenly the old mother doubled up as if she had stomach cramps, a shocked dialogue followed and the audience roared with laughter; my friend translator told me that the mother had become pregnant again. The bad couple were furious because there would be less food for them to eat, and the good couple offered to rear the child.

Seven years later their food crops were spoilt by floods and the old parents worried so much they died. The four remaining adults argued about who was now head of the family. They were now really having to shout because heavy rain was hammering on the roof of our corrugated iron theatre. I thought that the peasants would solve their problem and was surprised when the gods intervened. A man dressed as Tai Bei came down from the heavens with his attendants, and he took the seven-year-old boy as his student. But he left no message for the good foster parents, who were distracted with worry and began searching everywhere for the child. And that was how the play ended; a man stood up and blew an old silver trumpet and everyone got up to leave. No applause, no conclusion, no wrapping up of loose ends, I felt I'd been left in mid-air. Why hadn't the bad guy got what he deserved and the good guy been rewarded? Perhaps Part II would be on the morrow, but when I asked my friend he said no, that's the whole play and tomorrow they will perform it again. I watched the audience of minority people dispersing towards the countryside and decided that the following day I would take a country bus to see where they came from.

I had been told about a strange beauty spot in a region inhabited by the Sani people. The stone forest at Shilin isn't fossilised trees. The name comes from the tall limestone pinnacles, hundreds of them, which rise up so densely they form a forest. It's now a famous tourist spot, but you can get away from the crowds if you follow the smaller paths, some barely visible. One took me down along passages below ground level between slabs of rock, open to the sky but continually descending, growing narrower until I had to stoop double or squeeze through sideways. There was no specific ground level, it varied according to the debris of rock that has fallen from above over the millennia. There was hardly enough earth or light to support plants, yet a few hardy vines and clinging trees have taken root. Several times I thought that my path had ended but when I explored the side tunnels I found ways that led ever onwards, now into dark gloomy mossy dungeons with water dripping into pools. It was a relief when the path began to climb, and although I was frequently surprised at its obstacles, it finally emerged back into daylight.

Looking at my map didn't give me any clue where I was and I couldn't see any of the landmarks it described, so I began looking for a path leading upwards. Going upwards led me into a different world. Soaring pinnacles made shapes like cathedral arches. Fir trees in high crevices were stark outlines against the sky. Several vines and creepers, ablaze with red and pink flowers, sprawled over the tips of rock fingers. Small brown squirrels darted out of my way, and although sometimes I heard people's voices, I didn't see anyone until finally I emerged onto a sharp ridge overlooking the massif of the stone forest.

I stayed overnight at the tourist lodge in Shilin; I'd wanted to camp out but the mosquitoes were too desperate. Soon after dawn I returned to the forest as the mist rose slowly from the wet pinnacles, and the spiders' webs glistened in the early sun. It is easy to tell the less trodden paths by the number of unbroken webs across them. But while the place was deserted I enjoyed rambling around the main routes, going up to little pavilions and major view points. Their climbing handholds are worn to a polished smoothness. When I heard the coaches begin to arrive I went away.

In a village nearby I met a young woman of my own age, called Waree, who told me about some forthcoming celebrations for Ho-ba-jie (Flaming-torch festival). There would be dancing, singing and bull-fighting. We watched a bit of bull-fighting being practised, or rather, people trying to persuade two water-buffalo to fight each other. The trouble is, water-buffalo tend to be placid, agreeable creatures. One old bull had obviously had years of experience at this annual fight; he lowered his horns obediently and charged at his opponent. Wasting no time, his opponent fled. Waree was due to visit her mother, who lived in a village twenty miles away and she agreed to let me go along too. We went by bus, an old bus and in the rain its roof leaked so much that I was forced to put up my umbrella to keep dry. The local version of a mackintosh is made of palm-tree fibre, sewn with string into the form of a long-tailed jacket.

As a present for her mother Waree was carrying an armadillo. She kept it on a string, tied around its back and armpits, and when she lifted it, the armadillo curled up in a ball; brown and scaly, with its long snout tucked under its tail. When she put the bundle on the floor it uncurled to half a yard in length and scrabbled with long-clawed toes to get away. We spent the day at Waree's mother's village and didn't eat the armadillo. It was being kept for the feast of Ho-ba-jie. Waree and I gathered mushrooms which grow on the higher land. We collected various types with yellow gills and green domes and fat, dumpy, ball-shaped ones with brittle shells.

The following evening, back in Shilin, I watched a dancing

display which opened with some young women being called out into the open by young men and musicians. Each girl carried a bamboo pole with loose rattling studs on it, which hit the ground as they danced, accompanied by men playing flutes. Their singing was the customary high nasal tone which still sounded odd to me. But then I also find Italian opera an odd way to sing.

When they weren't singing their dances were more complex with quicker foot movements, hopping, stamping, and skipping from side to side, and waving their arms, which all tended to make their headdresses slide lop-sided. These confections were pillboxes with fins which stuck out upwards and sideways, giving an unusual effect, and for extra security some girls had tied them on with ribbons. The next dance was set to the plaintive notes of a flute and violin, with the girls trilling, calling out, and their hands making the motions of weaving cloth; then kneeling and stitching it with embroidery.

Lastly the young people launched into their famous tiger dance. Four men dance with twirling three-pronged pitchforks and, unknown to them, a two-man tiger comes along. It cavorts about and angrily shakes its papier mâché head, then sits down to scratch its striped coat, and lie quietly. At this moment four young women dance past on a fruit-picking errand, twisting the fruit off imaginary trees with grace and dexterity. The sound of the drums and three-string fiddles intensifies as the tiger makes ready to pounce. When the music reaches a frenzy the tiger leaps up, the girls flee, and the four men with pitchforks charge in to kill the tiger.

After the dance-performance I noticed Waree standing at the back of the crowd, and slipped over to say goodbye to her, since I would be leaving the area in the morning. She insisted on giving me an embroidered bag, and so I gave her my umbrella as a gesture of thanks for making my stay so enjoyable.

17   The Burma Road to Dali

The bus journey from Kunming to Dali used to take two days, but nowadays the drivers try to make it in one, which means they drive like demons for eleven hours around zigzagging mountain bends. This is the Burma Road, built during the Second World War, based on the mule track which has existed since antiquity. When Marco Polo came along the track it took him nearly two weeks from Kunming to Dali. We saw the remains of several accidents and traffic was surprisingly heavy, much of it being army convoys from the Burmese borderlands. It was a sunny day. The villages through which we passed were of mud and mud-brick. Gone was the drab concrete of Kunming. The hills had bamboo groves, and crops of rice, maize and tobacco. Most of the Chinese passengers dozed off to sleep, but with the bus swinging so violently around the hairpin bends one had to sleep with both hands holding on.

The Han woman beside me had stowed a string bag of pears on the overhead rack. The bag gradually slid through the bars and a pear fell out, hitting me on the head. The lady apologised and as she settled back another pear hit me. So I got up and re-tied the bag, feeling more fortunate than the man who'd been hit on the head by a falling metal water-bottle. There were several other foreigners on the bus; they were younger than those I'd met in the north-west of China, more like hippy-trail people extending their trip of the Far East to take in a taste of China. A student couple sat in the front seat, she on his lap, kissing and cuddling each other. It was a shame that they couldn't see what embarrassment this caused all around the bus, not only to the Chinese, who were shocked, but also to their fellow foreigners. As for me, I felt angry about it, because foreign women in China are well respected, but if local people see this kind of example they start getting funny ideas about us.

The girl was wearing short shorts, which many of the younger Western travellers in China seem to wear, not realising how this offends the local people's customs. What kind of Chinese woman would walk with bare thighs in public? I didn't want to share Dali with these people, and since I felt exhausted and irritable (I had developed a cough which grew worse and it kept me awake at nights) I decided to rest for two days in bed. The hotel in Dali had rats and its facilities were almost non-existent, but it was friendly and in the street behind it was the public bathhouse, which has marble baths. In the little I saw of Dali when I ventured out for a bath or a hot meal, much of the town seemed to be made of marble. Even some sidewalks and bridges are made of it.

My sickness got worse; my bones ached and I felt hot with fever. It was time to look for treatment. The choice lay between Western medicine, in a limited and unpractised fashion, or acupuncture, or herbal medicine, which has been traditional in China since early days. By making enquiries I discovered that one of Yunnan's most highly regarded herbal doctors was living in Dali. I found him at the herbal hospital, in a treatment room whose shelves were stacked with jars of dried leaves, roots and powdered concoctions. He wrote me a herbal prescription in Chinese, though I recognised the weights and measures prescribed in grams. In the dispensary the orderly weighed out some twigs, mushrooms, flowers and bark, and he told me to make tea with it three times daily.

Within a few days I felt strong enough for an outing by local bus to visit a Bai village – Dali used to be the capital of the Bai kingdom. The men are stonemasons, so their village on the side of Cangshan mountain is a handsome monument to their art, with stone dwellings tucked inside stone courtyards, and streams channelled below large flagstones which form the roads.

When I sat in the village square and began to write in my notebook I found myself being gradually edged up to by shy teenage girls, fascinated by my handwriting. Their language has no written form. If the educated Bai need to use writing, they use the Chinese ideographs. While the girls watched my script I had a close look at their headdresses – red and pink cloths in six layers built outward like a halo around their heads, using their long black plaits as a final layer. Strands of pink wool and white silken tassels at the back completed the effect. Their clothes were flamboyant red and pink corduroy waistcoats over white blouses, and over their trousers were floral aprons with silk fringes.

Some girls arriving from the fields with laden back-baskets paused to talk to their friends. I tested the weight of their baskets and guessed them to be between forty and sixty pounds.

For such a weight the basket is supported from a wide woven band across the girl's forehead. At this time of year, while transplanting rice, the unmarried girls look particularly fine because such displays are believed to please the natural forces which control the richness of a harvest. In the fields and paddies the girls' colourful attire makes them very noticeable, working on their haunches in scattered groups. While working they often call to each other in song. The replies come back in song; the songs' words are spontaneous and the girls carry on witty question and answer conversations, improvising as they go along. When girls and young men are courting they frequently make love songs together in the same way.

On market day (Monday) I caught a bus to Xingping, a short journey but the road was busy with traffic of ox-carts, pony-carts and taxi pony-carts going to the market. I arrived early and from the few stall holders already in position I managed to buy some hot, doughy molasses pancakes. For a leisurely breakfast I took them to a flat rock which formed part of a causeway from the marketplace across the marshes towards another village, and I sat watching the gentle flow of people arriving for market. Most were on foot, carrying large back-baskets or bundles on bamboo yokes. Some of the fishing baskets were larger than the people carrying them. They made interesting filigree silhouettes against the blue sky. A woman holding dozens of woven straw sandals stopped to stare at me. Whole dead pigs were being pushed along in handcarts. Live piglets ran riot and got their strings in a terrible tangle around their leader's legs. I tried not to laugh.

If the people had had any choice they wouldn't have walked past me (my camera was in action) but the causeway was too long and narrow for detours. The girls were particularly shy, the prettiest ones being the shyest. One who had to stop and adjust her load was wearing nine layers of headdress. The steady flow of people began to fill the marketplace. An early area of activity was the pig sale, which I went to watch for its entertainment value. Ten piglets on ropes lassooed a group of women, while men who had bought full grown pigs were attempting to drag the pigs away from each other. The pigs just dug in their toes and leaned back, but were hauled along regardless. The air was rent with squeals of protest; and the stronger pigs managed to pull their new masters off towards their old homes. It was a non-stop comedy. The most colourful section in the market was where young Bai girls were selling embroidery knicknacks, flamboyant and fluorescent wools and silks, tassles, gold thread and sequins.

That evening at my usual restaurant I shared a table with a couple of people I'd met in Kunming, a Hong Kong Chinese called Victor and a Dutch woman, Hanneke. It was the sort of busy informal restaurant where you might find the kitchen boy shampooing his hair under the tap in the back yard where the patrons sat, while another lad beheaded the chicken we had ordered and left it to reel its headless death throes on the flagstones in front of us. Victor wanted to visit Ju Jie Shan, a sacred mountain two bus-rides and a pony-cart-ride away from Dali. He knew how to get there and we agreed to meet early next morning. I felt fully recovered from my illness. I'd never been to a sacred mountain before, and this seemed the right moment.

18 The Sacred Mountain

After the two bus-rides, we still had about forty miles to go and over lunch considered the merits of a taxi rank of ponies, mules and donkeys drawn up before us. Neither Victor nor Hanneke are horsey people so it was left up to me to explain that we didn't want a donkey or a mule (too slow), we wanted a nicely-built pony with sturdy legs. Not wanting breakdowns I took a good look at the trimness of their feet. A secondary consideration was the type of cart. They were dogcarts, and although of course, springs were not on offer, we agreed we might need one with roll bars and a tarpaulin against probable rain. That only left a choice of two ponies with suitable carts, and since the driver of one was asking twice the recommended price we took the more honest taxi-man. When the deal was concluded we folded the cart's tarpaulin since the day was still sunny and hot, bundled our luggage on to the floorboards, climbed in on top, and set off without further delay. The pony trotted willingly with his ears pricked.

The air smelt of lemon geraniums which were being grown in the fields. Hanneke noticed that in the patchy blue horizon the only part obscured by dark rainclouds was the direction we were heading. But I was too happy to worry. Fences of sisal border fields of rice, maize, tobacco and pumpkins. The smell of lemon geranium got stronger and we came to a roadside boiler where the plants were being turned into syrup.

The pony had been trotting uphill for over an hour and he wasn't yet sweating. His driver said proudly that he had bought him as a six-year-old last year for 400 yuan (£132). He also told us that the sacred mountain is called 'Chicken Claw' because of its shape, and we should arrive there late that evening. The lane grew bumpier and steeper. In the bad patches we got out to walk, not merely to save the pony's strength but mostly because the cart was so uncomfortable. Going downhill the driver used a handbrake against one wheel, which squeaked loudly when applied; he made the pony keep trotting downhill and just used the brake to stop it being pushed into a gallop. On a flat stretch we pulled in to get out of the way of a three-horse chariot, driven at speed by a man standing upright on the cart. Actually that's probably more comfortable than bumping along on your bottom. He drove his team three-abreast, two ponies and a mule; and with bells clanging they galloped past raising a cloud of red dust, the Golden East's answer to Charlton Heston.

Out in the hills our lane wound through an army camp. It had a line of Howitzers and various installations. Soldiers were on parade and one group were doing an exercise of throwing hand-grenades using wooden dummy hand grenades. I got the feeling that we shouldn't be there, but no one shouted as we trotted through. And Victor assured me that he had asked in Dali for permission to visit this mountain, but he'd been told that permission was not necessary. Though of course this may be so for him, being Chinese, but not for Hanneke and me. The day was still hot and sultry. From the top of a small range we looked at the valleys and hilly basins ahead of us. At a distance the villages are particularly picturesque with their red-mud walls topped by straw from which grows a profusion of green weeds. Roofs are thatched and houses have rounded gables (like Dutch gables). In the lush rice valleys the air rang with the croaking of bullfrogs. Rice paddies were bordered by decorative plants which define the scalloped shapes of the hillside paddies. I enjoyed the way they fitted together like a jigsaw with odd-shaped pieces to fill in any gaps. The decorative edges are useful nitrogenous plants that revitalise the soil; though the farmers don't know this, they plant them because it is the custom.

At 4 p.m. we stopped in a village for a cup of tea. The villagers gathered thickly around the open-air café and those who couldn't see us climbed into trees to get a view. Their stares were not the blank stares of the average Han Chinese, their eyes were agog with curiosity. The driver told us that no foreigners had ever come up here before. Considering that Dali has only been open for a few months and this region is not on any trade route, it could easily be true. We climbed gradually higher until the fertile plains gave way to stunted bush and pine trees. Victor and Hanneke took a steep short cut while the pony-trap used the more slowly winding track. I stayed with the cart and when the driver settled back to light up his long-stemmed tobacco pipe, I took over the pony's reins. Calls of encouragement are 'Tor, har, sir,' and one can use the reins or stick to change the pony's direction. Show the whip on the right and the pony will move to the left. The only traffic we met was other pony carts, audible in advance by their bells; the ponies cantering two-abreast or in tandem, driven by standing charioteers. Tempting as it was to try it I knew that our luggage would bounce out of the cart at that speed.

When I asked the driver how much further it was to Shajie, he answered me in *li*, which is a Chinese unit of distance, more or less a kilometre, but it varies according to the type of terrain underfoot. The more difficult the route, the longer it will take. This made perfect sense to me. We caught up to Victor and Hanneke and I relinquished the reins to the driver since he would be able to drive faster and more safely than I. It would soon be dusk. Recent rain had made the track muddy and rutted. One more hilly pass and we began the descent on to the plain of Ju Jie Shan. We passed a shrine with incense burning on it, and at the foot of the hills we had to ford two rivers, rather deep and muddy, but the water didn't quite flood over the floorboards. At 7.30 we went through the old arched gate into Shajie. Although it's just a hamlet there was no problem over where to stay. Most Chinese villages had inns for the use of pilgrims and traders, and Shajie was no exception. We were charged one yuan each for beds. The rats were a nuisance but we hung our food supplies from hooks on the walls.

The innkeeper's daughter cooked supper for us. The first dish was of deep-fried leaves; they were obviously a delicacy and tasted deliciously nutty and crisp. These were followed by dishes of fried potato and aubergine, rather a greasy meal but filling enough. Then we sat around talking with some locals, one of whom played a bamboo flute. Twilight faded into pearly clouds beyond the wet tiles of the gatehouse roof. We asked if many pilgrims still visit Mount Ju Jie Shan, and they said that few come, though there are occasional groups of Hong Kong Chinese who have heard about the mountain and come to climb it. They told us emphatically that they had not seen a European here before.

At seven the next morning the three of us set out on a path up the lower slope of the mountain. Its summit was still not visible but the morning was misty. Trees dripped and spiders' webs glistened. We wondered what we might find on the mountain, since the only thing we knew was that there had once been 350 monasteries here with about 5,000 monks, but obviously that was in times past. Victor hoped there would be hermits and recluses, I thought there might be some ruins, and

Hanneke was not in a good mood so she disagreed with what we said but offered no alternative. She seemed to be having a problem with the altitude, but it would get worse as we climbed and I hoped she wouldn't run into difficulties. The path was rocky and slippery wet, and as we went on I could see that it had once been a cobbled track. Well-fitted stones still existed on some of the steeper gradients. At a crossing over a stream we noticed the ruined corners of a gatehouse, now almost indiscernible, hidden by moss and knotted ropes of vines. A mile further we came to where the stream had once been diverted to run under a building. It had holes at each side for water to channel through, and partial walls hidden beneath dense forest undergrowth. The next ruined building was a hut built into a massive tree's roots, with half the hut inside the hollow tree. Inset into the inner trunk was a clay fireplace, and the presence of a kettle showed that the place is sometimes still used.

Wild chrysanthemums, wild roses, bracken, archangels, and stinging nettles had overgrown much of the route, and there were side paths leading off at frequent intervals. We traced some of them, I found one which led to a waterfall, aptly named 'The Waterfall that Penetrates the Clouds'. The path levelled out and ran along under a cliff, we paused often to catch our breath, and after about four hours we saw the impressive gates of a monastery, its gatehouse guarded by two sculpted dragons breathing dark smoke from their nostrils and throwing flames from their paws. With excitement we discovered that the place was not empty or derelict, but still functioning. According to one of the monks, this 'blessed saint' monastery was created by a monk called Without Cloud, who had spent three years collecting enough money for it to be built. Its heyday was in the Ching Dynasty in the twelfth century and nowadays it has only nineteen monks and eleven nuns. Two of the nuns were young girls and the rest were old women wearing black woollen berets and blue tunic and trousers. One I talked with was seventy years old, her role was the daily cleaning of the temples, and one and a half hours of prayer and meditation from 5 a.m. She came originally from Dali, but said she had no wish to go back and live there, being content with her life on the mountain.

A hunchback in the kitchen made us lunch of rice, greens and egg with spicy chutney. Victor announced that he wanted to take some polaroid pictures of the monks to give them as presents, and they all hurried away to don their best robes.

Before we left the monks showed us a map of the sacred mountain that they had drawn and copied; it marked all the old monasteries so we asked which ones still existed but the monks just shook their heads. In turn we pointed to each marker and they replied 'gone, gone', right the way through except for a couple of temples near the top and the monastery on the summit. The cause of the general disaster was the Cultural Revolution, when religion had been seen as superstitious nonsense, to be wiped off the face of China. The extent of the damage was something we would see for ourselves.

The nuns assured us that even if we didn't find our way to the top, the sacred mountain has plenty to offer: 47 hills, 13 peaks, 34 cliffs, 45 caves, and over 100 streams. This litany showed how they care about their mountain.

We climbed on past a ruined monastery. Orange lilies grew up through the foundations. Our path was now a riverbed of slippery clay. Although we only carried lightweight packs we stumbled frequently and stopped for rests at ten-minute intervals, gasping in the rarefied air. Some ponies and donkeys laden with supplies came scrabbling their way up the path, and passed us, driven by two local men. They said that the top monastery was still several hours away. They were going to a nearby temple which was under reconstruction. As we passed it I peeked in to see what was happening. The temple was being renovated almost from scratch. Small statues were being built from wood and straw thickly plastered in mud. When the effigy is complete they jab holes in the mud so it won't crack as it dries. Three young artists were working on the face of a giant door-guardian, giving him a furrowed forehead, bushy eyebrows and angry snarl. The boys worked together without any squabbling about 'why aren't you doing the same as me?' They worked as a team and indeed needed no discussion because they used a standard type of features. I wondered why the temples are being restored; it must have been a Party decision, but the logic eluded me. Perhaps they genuinely wish to encourage Buddhism, or tourists? Though China has other more accessible Sacred Mountains.

Up and up we climbed, through fir-clad woodlands, with rhododendron bushes in white blossom and occasional views over the mountains and plains that we had crossed the previous day. While Hanneke had a rest to try to get acclimatised I scrambled around and had not gone very far along an overgrown path when I spotted the wall-foundations of more ruined temples, located below a magnificent cliff on a mountain shoulder. Old beams and timbers charred black informed me that the place had been burned down then smashed up; smashed up so thoroughly that I was surprised by the amount of violence that must have been used. The Cultural Revolution must have been an amazingly powerful force of destruction, to reach all this way south-west and obliterate nearly 350 monasteries on a remote mountain. Of this ruin, four archways are left, and the flights of steps up to a gatehouse which lies in rubble under ferny weeds. Through gaping cracks in the marble flooring grew purple and white ground-orchids and mauve-spotted lilies. Venus hair was in bloom with dainty leaves and even daintier purple star flowers. Buddleia, blue primulas and Michaelmas daisies also abounded. The forest has begun to close in over the ruins; from the branches hung trailing beards of tree moss and curtain-like drapes of grey-green filmy lichen.

We had ascended to cloud level and it began to drizzle with rain. I found temporary shelter in a deserted temple whose only occupant was a sculpted six-armed blue guardian. The blue was vivid indigo punctuated with red and white dots, and in his six arms he held a sword, some orbs, and a long serpent. Under his foot a demon squirmed with a pained and gasping expression, and across his chest was a string of eight plaster skulls.

Much as I liked Victor and Hanneke, they always seemed to be quarrelling. Hanneke's temper was made worse by her altitude problem and as twilight faded towards night we had to coax her up the last few yards to the summit monastery. We went into the gatehouse where a larger than life fat Buddha sat facing us, with laughter written in every line of his face; no doubt we were a laughable sight.

The old monk who greeted us in the inner yard didn't laugh, he seemed delighted to see us. He invited us in for tea, showed us where we could sleep on a straw pallet in a long stone hut, and during tea he told us about his life in this summit monastery. Now sixty-eight years old, he had lived here for fifty years, although he had run away to hide during the Cultural Revolution. Once he had taught fourteen novices, then none, and now he has one, a Kunming boy who joined him two weeks ago. We all sat up talking, smoke stinging our eyes, and when the time came for the monk's meditation he stayed with us, meditating yet throwing comments into our conversation from time to time. Most of the pilgrims who come here are Tibetan from southern Tibet, and some of the inscriptions are written in Tibetan script.

Finally exhausted, we retreated to the damp straw pallet with wet covers, and a copious number of rats. Somewhere along the line I had also picked up fleas. The itching awoke me soon after dawn and without hope of further rest I went out to look at the mountain-top. It's a rounded summit with cliffs dropping sheer from one side, and on the topmost point on the edge of the cliff stands a tall pagoda. With the dawn light and swirling mists it was almost ethereal. I rambled around watching as the mists parted giving glimpses of the mountains below, until, thoroughly chilled, I went back for a breakfast of greens, potatoes, rice and mushrooms. After eating we gave some money to the monastery and began a slow descent. Victor and Hanneke picked up their bickering where they had left off the night before. I didn't want to listen to their recriminations, so made my own way down slowly and alone. At the highest spring on the mountainside I stopped to drink. The water comes out below a large bulbous rock that has a stone tablet inscribed with a poem. All the odd natural formations on the mountain-side sport some small decoration, and large hollow trees have stone cairns and red cloth streamers, as befits consecrated nooks where gods and spirits are believed to dwell. Nature-worship is worship in a broad sense, it's more of a practice of preserving man's harmony with the spirit world, and keeping away the demons by showing respect and making offerings to avert their potential malice. One side path led me to the shack temple where a very untidy man was living. He wasn't communicative so we shared an amicable silence.

Rambling back down the path, I felt so happy in my solitude that I began feeling guilty for leaving my companions, so I caught up with them and spent the rest of the descent trying to make them be nice to each other. From Shajie we rented a pack-pony and walked to Binchuan, which marked the parting of our ways. At sunset from the hotel balcony in Binchuan I could see the pagoda atop the Sacred Mountain, forty miles away, backed by a silvery sunset.

19 Yangtse rapids

Three days later I stood where a road crossed a tributary of the Yangtse that I'd reconnoitred. I clambered a short way up the rocky gulley to unfold and inflate my canoe. My intention was only to spend three or four days paddling downriver, just to see how it would be. My luggage was minimal; I'd left most of it at Dali and only carried my sleeping bag and billycan which all fitted under the canoe's spray cover. After a final check that I'd left nothing behind, I paddled away downstream. It felt good to be back on the water. From the rocky gulley the river flowed across a flat plain; its current was placid, the day was warm and sunny, and I paddled lazily, being in no hurry. When I stuck my paddle upright in the river to test its depth, it was only a yard deep but gluey with mud. The earthen riverbanks were low enough at times for me to see out across fertile flatness cultivated with emerald green rice, and some maize plots that had golden heads of sunflowers showing above the maize plants. I passed near several small villages set well back from the stream; their presence was detectable in advance because each has an irrigation and household water channel branching off the river.

I stopped to stretch my legs. The muscles I'd used for the mountain-trek were feeling more sore now that they were having a rest. I strolled and watched some women bent over in rice paddies, busy thinning out the shoots and making bundles of the excess ones for replanting in fresh paddy-fields. New paddies were being rotavated by water-buffalo belly-deep in mud, and struggling to pull spiked wooden drums. In muddy pools near the river I paused to watch the resting buffalo wallow. They just sit there with only their heads and horns above water. Some children saw me, and stood rooted to the spot, round-eyed. When I moved they all ran away.

After a few miles the stream took me under a small arched stone bridge and, leaving the valley, flowed into a gorge. My mind woke up and I checked around for problems, but the gorge seemed quiet and the river, though rocky, was no larger or faster than before. Parts were overhung with shady trees, giving temporary relief from the sun, hot now at mid-afternoon.

Ahead I could hear foaming water, and felt the canoe begin to gather speed. As we came around a corner I saw rocks poking out of the water, but they were well-spaced and easy to avoid, making very minor rapids. The canoe rode them without trouble, responding well to my paddle-steering, so I stopped worrying. None of the rapids was above a Class 1 or 2 so I couldn't congratulate myself on achievement. But just to be sure I pulled over to the bank several times and got out to take a better look at what lay ahead. I gave myself a scare at the top of one swift rocky section when a deceptively strong eddy pushed the canoe broadside against two rocks, and the current roughed up against us. For a moment, things got serious but, digging my paddle fiercely backwards and throwing my weight on to the canoe's high side, I managed to free the prow and slid safely between the rocks. The moment made me cross with myself; a professional would never have let it happen.

Late afternoon sun lit the gorge, and its boulder-strewn banks glowed an earthy red. At a guess I had paddled twelve miles when we reached the junction where the small river joined a larger one, three times its size. The junction was not turbulent and I avoided the eddies, but straight away I could feel the increased power of the current. It made me suspect that we were in for some action. But not today; my muscles ached with tiredness, and I decided to stop and make camp for the night. An enclave among boulders and trees provided me with shelter, and the rocks would stay warm long into the cold night. I didn't bother to cook supper, having brought plenty of cereal and fruit. More than anything I wanted to lie down and sleep.

The next morning, after re-stowing my luggage and settling myself in the canoe, I paddled out into the turbulent current. The gorge was growing deeper and craggier. Where numerous large boulders had rolled down into the river the water heaved around angrily. I could usually hear roaring water long before I reached its cause; it was a case of working out exactly where was the focus of noise, because from down at river level I couldn't see the sudden drops and chutes.

In one fast patch a broad but invisible rock, causing a slide and trough of churning water, came so quickly that I went straight into it. The water roared, and the canoe was pulled sharply down on one side, though luckily it bobbed back up. But I was still in the trough which held us in its recycling path; with water pouring back on itself, making what canoeists call stopper waves and holes. I was in a hole.

The canoe didn't flip over simply because I was paddling so fast to both sides that it kept us nosing out of the hole. And equally abruptly we were free, racing away downriver; into some rocky turbulence and chutes which were rather fun. Running them gave me a tremendous thrill, a sense of exhilaration which is timeless. The gathering speed of the current made me hope that I hadn't taken on more than a sensible person would do. It's not necessary to kill oneself; neither to be so cautious that risk is nil. It's a question of striking the right balance for oneself. Knowing myself to have a reckless streak I try to be prudent. Before coming to China, my experience of rapid-filled rivers was limited to two trips; one using an inflated tyre-tube down the whitewater of a small highland river in Papua New Guinea, and the second in that same country, when I joined a team of professional river-runners with Avon rubber boats. We were attempting to make the first descent of the Wahgi River, one of the world's roughest whitewater rivers and it was filmed by BBC television, as part of their *River Journeys* series. The rapids we'd shot there were far larger than what I now tackled, but they had given me a taste for more.

In the afternoon the gorge became wilder, leading me into a wonderful landscape of rugged mountains. Their slopes were too rocky for much cultivation though occasionally there were stone cottages on hill shoulders. River bends became more frequent and they held bigger rapids. At most of them I had to stop and try to plan a way through. Easy in theory, but when I'm back down there paddling it I forget the order of what I'd planned to do, and there's so little time to think. I made one portage around a rapid which would have been a suicide-run, carrying the canoe under one arm and my baggage under the other.

Where the current swung beside a cliff-edged bend the canoe was suddenly swept into the cliffs. The nose hit first and I backpaddled for all I was worth, but was pushed sideways into an ugly maelstrom of currents. For an instant I remembered how this same thing had happened on the Wahgi expedition. We'd gone up against a wall and flipped upsidedown, which had given me my first swim through rapids. I was determined that the same wouldn't happen this time, and it lent strength to my efforts. Spray engulfed me as waves broke around rocks, and deep troughs yawned to both sides, but emerging from it we floated out on to calm water. Perhaps I'd been lucky this time and I wondered if the river spirits were looking kindly on me.

The small airleaks that my canoe had developed were not actually pinpricks, they were leaky valves, my fault because the valves had got sand stuck in them. So I accepted it as normal that one stops fairly often to pump up the canoe, as well as to scout rapids.

That night I camped, feeling too tired to care about making myself very comfortable, and falling asleep long before the sky was dark. In the night I awoke and wondered where on earth I was, until, on remembering, my sleepy senses relayed an abstract feeling which at first I couldn't identify, then I recognised it, it was happiness, the purely spontaneous joy of merely being part of the night.

The following morning began misty and I progressed downriver munching some breakfast. As the canoe rounded a bend I caught sight of the confluence of my river with another even larger river. A short time later we were projected out into the confluence which looked more like a sea, with water stretching in several directions to distant mist-blurred banks. I pondered which way led downstream; I couldn't remember and it was impossible to tell from the circling currents. The canoe was swept right out into the middle and we were caught in such a current that I had no control, but didn't know where I wanted to go anyway. The thunder of the water around was overpowered by the much greater thunder of water slightly distant. On the far horizon I noticed a long road bridge, but it came no closer, my canoe was going in a parallel direction; I wished we were nearer to the shore.

I began paddling forward hurriedly, since going back was clearly impossible and I felt anxious to be out of the middle. But for an agonising amount of time the far bank stayed barely visible through the mist, while the thunder of falling water grew louder beyond the road bridge. Slowly I realised that a large river bay had been created by the convergence of the two rivers, and that my canoe was being swept into it. After a hasty look at my map I knew that we had now joined the Upper Yangtse. My canoe went with the eddying flow into the vast bay, and when we reached the back of it I pulled in to the shore and prepared to take a look downriver on foot. From the basin the river plunges into a narrowing gorge where the water is stupefying in its power. It gave me the horrors so I packed up the canoe – only roughly since I hoped to use it again a few miles downriver – and I waited by the roadbridge for a truck or bus to come along. A truck came and gave me a lift along the road towards Lijiang, which has a reputation of being a fascinating place, though no one that I met had managed to get there.

From the front seat of the truck I had a good view as the road snaked up into a mountain range, and down again to the next massive bend in the river. The truck-driver wasn't talkative, the road demanded all his attention as it twisted and turned above cliff-hanging heights. Where the road came back near the river it was a less turbulent stretch and I decided to try canoeing again. The truck-driver couldn't understand why I wanted to get out in the middle of nowhere, so I explained that I was a botanist making a study of local plants.

Back on the river my canoe bounced around like a cork. I paddled close to the shore, for although there are more rocks there, the current is fractionally slower and I wanted the reassurance of land nearby. It was encouraging to see from the seasonal watermarks high up the banks that the river was not yet in its most violent season.

The first major rapid had a complex layout of rocks; I had to paddle hard left to get through a smooth chute then quickly right to avoid a nasty-looking stopper hole that seemed to cover half the river. Beyond it were various groups of rocks. I scouted it on foot before attempting it by canoe. The mist had not cleared and was developing into fairly thick fog. The canoe made it through the first part and around the hole; I was paddling hard and stayed well in control. But one of the blades on my paddle came loose (maybe its connector was still greasy with yak-butter, or perhaps I'd been cautious about making it too tight). The blade slid helplessly in the current and I was afraid it would be torn off the handle. Rocks passed on both sides with others up ahead. I paddled one-sided, trying to grab at the loose blade in each open stretch, and when the canoe hit a rock I thought we were done for. The rebound sent us into a small stopper wave but the next instant I was on top of the wave, riding it, and paddling like a one-armed windmill at full speed until the canoe slid forward off the wave and I managed to pull in to the shore and re-tighten the blade.

The fog had thickened patchily. We passed under a footbridge and made several portages around impassable rapids. On one occasion I tried lining the canoe through, which means tying nylon ropes to it and letting the current carry it through as you walk along the bank. The problem of the rope trick was that as the current took the canoe downriver I couldn't hold on to it. The nylon rope started to burn through my fingers. I yelled, 'Stop, stop,' but couldn't stop. My hands felt burned raw. In a last-ditch effort to avert disaster I pulled the rope around a rock and wrapped it round again to take the strain. The current fought the canoe, and I stood helplessly for a moment watching as it flipped over upsidedown. Leaping down on to a rock, I hauled the canoe sideways toward the bank before the rope could break. To my immense relief it came out of the current and drifted to shore downstream of the rock. Everything seemed still in place but my camping gear was soaked.

Without sunshine it wasn't worth stopping to dry out my things, and since the river had become steadier, I continued paddling downstream. Thinking about all the accidents I'd had over these past three days made me wonder if I was being accident-prone. But I told myself stoutly this was the Yangtse and it was no baby. Shortly afterwards, while surveying a rapid far larger than the one I'd just avoided, I decided to try paddling it. The size and power of its numerous chutes was slightly terrifying but the layout wasn't difficult. An exciting run, at the first ledge the river dropped me into a mill-race of currents, then through a neck and into the mainstream. Going at speed, I steered the canoe into the next chute, dead centre, and went into the V-waves that followed it. Five sets of V-waves towered above me. The canoe rode them almost sideways and my paddle was stroking air not water. The largest chute was still ahead, far larger than anything this canoe had tried before. Too late to back out, I stopped paddling and clung on to the canoe. It raced down the chute and plunged into the chaos below. Water came pouring in from both sides, but I told myself that inflatable boats cannot sink. More water poured in as we shot the last part of the rapid. The canoe was virtually under the surface. But I was still sitting there, thrilled to have made it through in one piece, though wishing that I'd brought a bailing can. Paddling a waterlogged canoe is heavy work and I aimed for the nearest shore. In the shallows I slid out of the canoe and upturned it to drain out the water; much easier than bailing cans.

Occasionally as I continued downriver I noticed a bus or truck crawling along the mountain road. They were going to Lijiang; the road would soon veer away to the west. If I wanted to visit Lijiang it was almost time to make the decision. Ahead the river grew yet steeper, but I didn't want to stop. Common sense tried to assert itself. And I reminded myself that I wasn't trying to prove or achieve anything. The afternoon sky had turned stormy, my sleeping gear was already soaked, and my head ached every time I moved it too quickly. And perhaps I was frightened of what lay ahead. So I packed up and walked out quickly before I could change my mind.

20   Invitation to the waltz

It took me two very exhausting hours to walk up the side of the gorge, but soon after reaching the road I got a lift to Yongshan which is on the way to Lijiang. The driver wore a fur hat with earflaps and the other passengers were country girls with baskets full of freshly-picked fungi. Yongshan is in the borderland between the Bai and the Norsu people, who used to have a bad reputation for their ferocity and wild ways. They were a pocket of the past, isolated by a loop in the Upper Yangtse, high on the edge of the world's roof. The only contact they had with the outside, until they were communised, was when they swooped down to the plains and attacked villages for loot and slaves. The slave raids went on into the 1940s. You can tell some of the former landowners from the ex-slaves by their black turbans – slaves wore white ones.

At the evening market in the village square there was a motley mixture of peoples including some women in very distinctive black headdresses: starched cloth squares stuck out like mortarboards with the front either jutting straight out or, for younger women, it was bent down over their forehead.

On the way back to the inn where I was staying I met a woman who wanted to show me something. She pulled me by the hand to her house and called a girl to come out. The girl had hair as blonde as mine. She was only eight years old, and she looked at me with the kind of amazement that the ugly duckling must have shown on its first encounter with swans like itself.

Supper was good. I shared a table with three men, two Bai and a Naxi, and after eating, they accompanied me to the candlelit night market. That night as I retired to bed there was a knock on the door, my new friends had arrived with a party of their friends. Men, women and children, more kept arriving and although I shut the door a few times, people continued to come in until the room was packed. Some late arrivals were old women who said they hadn't had the chance to look at me earlier and that they hoped I wouldn't be upset by their curiosity. We communicated in a melange of Bai, Han, English and sign language; my photographs were shown around the room and a good time was had by all. When I finally settled down to sleep I gave thanks for not being in a wet sleeping bag; the bed's mattress was hard but dry, and the bedbugs were not as bad as they'd been in other places.

Next morning I caught the 7 a.m. bus to Lijiang. It was a three-hour ride up over a series of ridges, empty and magnificent; the only signs of humans were the paths on mountainsides, red lines across green grassiness. A chain of lakes edged by weeping willow trees stretched up through the valleys. We emerged on to a plateau then continued rising. Finally the road began to descend and the bus coasted at great speed down to Lijiang, situated on a plain at the foot of Yunnan's biggest mountain, Mount Yulung, 18,000 feet. The town itself was not the quaint place I had imagined. It was a mass of ugly modern concrete buildings, and busy with more construction works in progress. So I hitch-hiked out of town, heading north on a dirt road. I wasn't planning to go far, just to visit some Naxi villages and a wall of ancient paintings that I'd seen marked on an old map. Honeysuckle climbed in the hedgerows, and in the villages there were sunflowers and Michaelmas daisies. The day was warm and summery and, apart from having leaden legs, I felt light-hearted.

The people I met were friendly but no one had heard of the wall paintings. Unfortunately my knowledge of Naxi language is limited to hello (n-er go-le), drink (ter-chua) and thank you (yerbe), which I'd learned on the bus. But I happened to be carrying a small paintbrush in my handbag. At first my mime was greeted with puzzled expressions, then an elderly man guessed what it was about, and he instructed some boys to take me to a temple. But it was locked. The search for its key took me to the house of a 'barefoot doctor' who told me that the temple's guardian had gone to Lijiang for the afternoon. He invited me to stop and drink tea, and as my original purpose seemed thwarted, I relaxed and made friends with him. The term 'barefoot doctor' does not refer to his feet, it means rather that he is barely qualified as a doctor. His training of three to six months qualifies him to deal with the basic essentials; first aid, minor ailments, hygiene and health care. He also knows a little about acupuncture and Chinese herbal medicine. The 'barefoot doctor' system is excellent in a land where doctors are in short supply. The instruments I could see on this doctor's shelves included a large old-fashioned syringe, many pill bottles, some forceps, and various bits of plastic tubing.

While we sat chatting and drinking tea in the courtyard, a sick man lying in a handcart was wheeled into the yard. The doctor examined him, wrote a prescription and gave him an injection, using the half-pint syringe. I turned away because I can't bear to watch injections, and rested my eyes on some flowering hollyhocks and chrysanthemums beside the white-washed yard walls. Bees hummed, it was a moment of suspended time.

The local medicine here in the pre-communist era had been based more on magic than science. Healing the sick often involved animal sacrifices, invocation of spirits, and divination using chicken bones. Shamans could be male or female. Their work was to drive out the demons that caused diseases and bad luck, yet prevent man's soul from leaving his body prematurely. In this region, dead people were represented by ancestor baskets that contained a small bamboo tube, in which the dead man's soul was believed to dwell. Of Marco Polo's legendary elixir of life, for immortality or longevity, I could find no trace.

A pleasant young man helped me find a hotel not too far from the bus station, as I intended to be off to Dali first thing in the morning to collect the rest of my luggage. As I was getting ready for bed there was an insistent knocking on my door. It was the pleasant young man and a young woman who said they were both from the police. She could speak some English, but apologised for her inadequate command of it. So I congratulated her good accent and launched into small talk. Like the man, the woman also had a lovely face and charming manners. We talked idly for ten minutes before she managed to ask where I'd come from. In reply, I gave her the bus ticket showing that I would be leaving Lijiang at 7 a.m.

She told me that Lijiang is closed. 'Closed,' I repeated the word several times to make sure we were talking about the same thing. 'You mean it's not open?' When she assured me that this was so, I apologised profusely for having made such a mistake. Also I said that Lijiang is beautiful and the people so good, and asked when it was likely to open to foreigners. Our conversation didn't go along the lines she'd planned. It was frustrating for the policewoman when she couldn't make me understand her questions, and it meant that she was losing face. Over the next hour she continued to lose face though I kept congratulating her on her accent and the meeting stayed sincerely amicable.

I had confessed to my mistake, but the two police couldn't decide what punishment to levy. They conferred quickly in Chinese. I suggested that my penalty should be to leave and not return until the year the town becomes open, leaving by the 7 a.m. bus. The policewoman was only too glad to finish our meeting and escape further loss of face. On their way out they arranged for the hotel receptionist to give me a wake-up call at 6 a.m.

My pillow was stuffed with grain, all the pillows were, but it wasn't uncomfortable and I slept well. When I arrived at the bus station I'd just got time to buy some steamed buns before boarding the bus. It would be a six-hour journey, though luckily I had a window seat.

We had now left the Naxi region and were back among the Bai who have lived in this area for over 3,000 years. The villagers were harvesting wheat, and had an ingenious method of threshing it. They spread the wheatsheaves thickly across the tarmac road so the traffic had to run over them. At first I didn't understand what was happening and why people kept dashing into the road to rake their wheat into our path. Then I saw others gathering up the crushed straw and collecting the ears of wheat into drying trays. The traffic was being used as a thresher.

After five hours I noticed clouds of smoke coming from a hill, and some groups of women carrying gongs, drums and offerings. 'Stop, stop, I want to get out,' I told the bus-driver, and he obligingly stopped, though he warned me that I might not find another bus to Dali that day. Making my way to the headland I found crowds of Bai people, many of them kneeling in semi-circular groups. They were making a clackety rhythm with Bai-type percussion instruments and a woman in the centre of each group beat cymbals or big drums. More people were joining the groups and they began to form a procession, heading for the top of the hill. Their welcoming smiles encouraged me to join them.

The path was stony and steep. I walked up beside an old lady and helped by carrying her tray of offerings. On it were balanced some tiny teacups of rice, cooking oil, tobacco and a colourless drink. The path zigzagged steeply and as the women climbed they sang and made music. Their shoes were embroidered slippers with upturned toes. Almost everyone wore their traditional blue costume and bonnet, with jewellery of jade bracelets, earrings, and clusters of silver ornaments and lucky charms hanging down their backs.

On reaching the crest we found dozens of small, improvised shrines surrounded by trays of offerings: pork, plums, apples, potatoes, and crunchy bread-puffs coloured bright red, green and yellow. Joss sticks and large coils of incense smouldered all over the ground, and decorated shapes of paper were continuously being added to fires to keep them alight. I watched a woman offering a chicken, lifting it up high over the shrine, facing outwards over the open green valley and the rushing river. She offered the bird upward six times then took it away to prepare it for the cookpot.

After finding some women who could speak Chinese I learned that the ceremony was to commemorate the death of an important man in their society. All the women relations of his extended family and his village had brought offerings. Many people invited me to sit and rest with their groups and among them I met an old lady who knew a smattering of English, and also knew how to waltz. Her English and my Chinese weren't enough to discover where she'd learned to dance, but she showed me her steps, then clasping me around the waist with one arm and pushing my arm out ahead of us tango-style, she began to sing a rousing tra-la-la tune. She insisted we dance, to let the Bai people see a waltz. So we waltzed.

21 The Dragon Boat Race

The day of the Dragon Boat Race began for me at 5.30 a.m. when the innkeeper slaughtered a pig outside my bedroom door. The squealing was enough to awaken the dead, and I opened my door on to a courtyard that ran with blood. I had come from Dali by ferry across Lake Er Hai to the village of Haidong for the annual Ho Ba Jie festival. The Dragon Boat Race would be a highlight of the ceremonials. Haidong wasn't marked on my alien's permit and I had feared they would turn me off the ferry, but in the event everyone was too busy to make an issue of it.

The race was not due to start until the afternoon but all through the morning many gaily decorated boats arrived in Haidong's bay. From the cliffs I watched sailing junks, their tall rectangular sails taut with the wind as they rounded the point. Occasionally I heard snatches of song coming from men and women crews. The dragon boats were painted with dragons and flowers; there were red and gold flags fluttering from their masts, and as they came in to moor they let off strings of firecrackers. More firecrackers could be heard in the village and when I walked through it there were mounds of flaming straw being used to singe off pigs' bristles. Five more pigs were being prepared to feed the crowds who were invited from other villages around the lake. Market stalls were set up in lane crossroads and along the village waterfront, selling things like hot sweet buns and roasted pine cones with delicious pine nuts inside. The sellers and buyers were mostly Bai girls dressed in their Sunday best. Shocking pink abounded. Babies and toddlers were wearing red bonnets of different styles studded with silver decoration; one bonnet framed the baby's face like a sunburst of triangles, some had ear-whorls, or pompoms on springs, many had protuberances like horns, or prows at the crown and neck upcurling and strung with extra silver chains.

Stopping to buy a snack I made the mistake of choosing a doughy pancake that was filled with crushed chilies. They nearly burned the roof off my mouth and it took four cups of cold tea to revive me. In the village square a fencing match had begun with a spirited display by two men, then by two women.

The latter were fiercer and more aggressive, and each lunge was accompanied by cries of 'Hai, heh, ha', and an intent catlike narrowing of the eyes. Eight men in flowing robes leapt into the fray wielding long rapiers. At first they battled in pairs, thrusting, lunging, retreating, battling across the ground so fast that the crowd, myself included, fell back in a wave to avoid the blades slashing out around us. One pair were so ferocious they cleared the arena, and even when the smaller man dropped his sword he fought on, using Wushu techniques that I'd seen practised in Kunming, kicking the taller man in the chest. He jumped the blade as it slashed underneath him, and dodged, jumping and kicking, until finally grabbing his fallen rapier he 'killed' his opponent.

At noon a bugle call rang out to tell the boat crews to make ready and the crowd moved down to the lakeshore. Six boats representing six lakeside villages were each manned by seventy to eighty men, with two or three men to each oar. The oars were twelve feet long with small square paddle-blades. The race course was marked by buoys and flags, starting near the village shore and running across the bay to the temple point, where the boats had to go around the last buoy and return the same way. They would run in two heats of three with a final race between the two winners.

All six boats began by rowing a lap of honour. To try to keep their strokes in time each boat had a gong tied to its mast, and a man to beat out the rowing tempo; for encouragement they also had flute musicians and firecrackers on board. The boats moved ponderously, their long oars dipping slowly and evenly into the water, and were steered by a plank of a rudder with two men at the helm. Behind the six dragon boats came a flotilla of followers, jockeying for good positions where they could drop anchor and watch the race. It was a hot sunny day, I sat with crowds of villagers on the cliffs. Unfortunately the summer's breeze gradually became a wind and by the time the first race started the wind was fierce and the waves were a mass of white-cresting rollers. As the starting-gun fired the oarsmen scrabbled frantically with their oars at the water, few keeping time with the gongbeat, tangling their oars together, and looking from a distance more like drunken galloping centipedes. A green-vested team drew ahead, working slightly in unison. Spray flew from their thrashing oars and from the waves crashing into the wooden prow. Once the boats had rounded the end flags they had the wind behind them. They surfed forwards, the green one was still ahead but a boat with two yellow dragons on its sides was making a late challenge.

Each race brought enormous excitement and the oarsmen took part with such enthusiasm that several oars got broken as they smashed together in leggy tangles. The final winner was the blue-vested team from Haidong, whose relative skill gave them the well-earned prize of 200 yuan (£60). As soon as the race was over, the ferries which had brought people from all around the lake began hooting to warn passengers of their departure. I hadn't realised there would be a Dali ferry but was glad to stay an extra night in Haidong, especially since the ferry would be full to capacity. People couldn't wait for the gangplank, they waded into the water and swam around while friends already on board tried to pull them aboard too. I hadn't noticed any other European people at the race, and one of the Dali boys told me that although a few tourists had tried to come they had no permits and had not been allowed on to the ferry. It made me realise how fortunate I was to have come early. Perhaps I was the first foreigner to see the Dragon Boat Races on Lake Er Hai.

On my return to Dali I fell into trouble with the security police, partly for having been across the lake, which they told me was closed. When they asked to see my alien's card I pulled it out of my pocket and some old bus tickets fell out with it. The policeman picked them up, and unfortunately for me, among them were the tickets I'd used on my journey to the Sacred Mountain. That heralded a five-hour session at the security office. They were polite but insisted that I write an official confession. My confession was duly made, with my apologies for my error. I certainly hadn't meant to break the law. They explained that only the township of Dali was open and that no side-trips of any description were allowed. The Sacred Mountain had never been open to foreigners.

22 Paddling into a watercolour

My time in China was running out now. The school holidays had arrived and packed the already crowded trains to insufferable capacity and beyond. Some students wanted to try out their schoolbook English on me, which can be boring unless you take a firm hold of the conversation yourself. I asked them how many Chinese characters they could write. They thought about 3,000, but admitted a well educated man would know 5,000. That is out of a total of over 40,000 characters. Characters, they explained, stand for ideas or concepts behind the words. Some single characters have over thirty-five strokes. The student told me that the Party tried to introduce a simplified version of Chinese script in 1978 but it didn't work because removing strokes left too many characters ambiguous.

One beauty spot I didn't want to miss was Huangguoshu, about which I hadn't been able to get any information on the grapevine. It seemed that no one bothered to stop there because you had to be able to speak Chinese to get to it, several hours on dirt roads south of Anshun. The only train to Anshun arrives there at 4 a.m.

I disembarked into an empty, dark and shadowy station yard. My brain was fuzzy with sleep, but I managed to cross town to the rural bus depot and dozed in a yard where two tramps were prowling. But they left me alone, and by 6 a.m. the townsfolk were beginning their day. A bus took me through tropical countryside with stone villages inhabited by minorities called Black Miao, White Miao, Flowery Miao, Rocket and Longtailed Miao, their names taken from their traditional headdresses. Huangguoshu village is perched on the rim of a river canyon looking straight at the largest waterfall in Asia. It earns the title for its sheer height and volume, which mesmerised me. I went down the cliff walk to the pool at the foot of the falls. The sun blazed down and the spray from the thundering water soaked me and created a double rainbow. A Chinese tour group arrived, carrying umbrellas. Their guide told me that today was a special day because a new cave walk behind the waterfall had been opened to the public. Her tour would be the first ever to go through it and I was welcome to join them. A pathway led us downstream to a bridge across the lower pool and back along the opposite cliff, reaching the falls at a point half-way up its side.

As we entered the cave-passage the guide noticed that there were no electric lights, despite the presence of an insulated power line which should have connected a series of lights for us to see our way through the tunnels. Either it had not yet been turned on or it was already broken. She asked if the group would prefer not to try it in the dark, but even the middle-aged Chinese ladies were adamant that they wanted to make the attempt. Between the ten of us we had one torch. The passage-way led into the cliff then steeply down some iron steps; it wasn't wise to use the powerline as a handrail in case it was live. My companions squeaked and squealed at some of the crevices we had to squeeze through, and the stalactites which caught our heads unawares. One had to feel almost every inch of the way; sometimes my hands encountered wonderful cauliflower shapes of cold rock. Feeling the way like this made for slow progress and when the line got halted by obstacles up ahead the human traffic jam stood hunched and bent double in a knobbly corridor, still chattering merrily while cold drips of water trickled down the backs of our necks. Natural holes in the tunnel led out behind the fall; the force of water rushing past our noses was awesome. Pits, puddles, steep steps, and pitch-dark passages. They echoed with the roar of water, and as we progressed we found more openings on to precipices behind and between the chutes. Rainbows abounded. By now I was soaked through, but didn't mind.

It took about half an hour from the start until we emerged into the dazzling sunshine on the other side of the waterfall. A man came hurrying down a path and spoke to our guide. If I'd been her I'd probably have burst out laughing at what he said, but she being Chinese, looked embarrassed as if she'd lost face. He had asked if we wanted the electric lights turned on! Apparently the switch was at his end.

This region is 'the land of waterfalls'. There are over seventeen major falls and I went to visit several of them. One was inside a cave system and approached by rowing-boat. Upriver from Huangguoshu was a good area for some canoe exploration; the river had interesting ledges and mini-falls, enjoyable because I didn't mind getting wet.

When I returned to Anshun to catch the 4 a.m. train I had got off three days earlier I experienced the typical China travel problem of being refused permission to sleep at the station hotel, so I said I'd wait on a bench. Someone told me to ask the luggage office for a key to the VIP waiting room, but the luggage clerk said there's no such thing. An hour later the hotel keeper offered me a room and also the luggage clerk came over with the VIP room key. Even though I should by now have got used to the contradictions in Chinese dealings with foreigners, they still took me by surprise.

The train arrived punctually, and was so crowded that I had to sit on my luggage in the aisle. People kept warning me that anything left unattended would be stolen. The express took twenty hours to Guilin; it grew rather oppressive as the temperature outside soared to a hot and muggy 100°F. We were nearly down to sea level. The Guilin area is famous for its scenery of weirdly eroded peaks, crystal streams and caverns. It has been renowned among travellers and artists for many centuries.

At a village called Yangdi I put my canoe into the Lijiang River which flows through the most beautiful part of the landscape and pulled on my floppy brimmed sun-hat. Water-buffalo wallowing in the shallows foraged underwater, long tendrils of water grasses trailing from their mouths as slowly they raised their heads to watch me pass. Behind the shores the land became craggier with tall, steep-sided hillocks. Pine trees grew from fissures in the rock. The river current was very slow and I suspected I was getting nowhere fast. It felt good. In calm bays the fishermen had strung their nets. One man on a raft was throwing a circular net with professional expertise. Fishermen here also use trained cormorants to help catch fish. The birds usually wear collars to prevent them swallowing their catch.

I spent two days making idyllic progress down this river. The sun would burn off the mist, evaporating it into a hot blue sky. I pulled my sun-hat over my face and floated for a while midriver, updating my diary. Various insects landed on the canoe, a black dragonfly which folded its four wings back and went to sleep; two red and green shiny beetles and some strange housefly-grasshopper creatures that landed on my paddle. We reached the junction of a tributary and the wonderland continued with pinnacles and sharks' teeth ridges, while the shores became sandy beaches backed by bamboo groves. A village loomed on the opposite bank. Women were out pounding their washing on the rocks. The whole scene reminded me of an ink and wash painting, with the ripples of water ruffling its surface. The local river traffic was bamboo rafts, each made from five bamboo poles turned up at the ends to float better, and propelled punt-style by men with long bamboo poles. Some rafts en route to a market were overladen and awash, but their cargoes were safely above waterlevel in a series of baskets. Clusters of fishing barges were moored near riverside villages; many fishermen live on their boats, which are spacious plank-hulled craft with curved awnings of wood or straw matting. Their fishing nets were strung to dry among washing lines of laundry, stacks of firewood and exotic song-birds in cages.

The worst hazard was caused by the motor cruisers which came ploughing their way along at top speed, travelling in convoys but trying to overtake each other, and some of them towing extra barges on long tow ropes. It gave me quite a shock when I saw an armada bearing down on me, their leaders blasting their air-horns to warn me to move over. The cruisers plied the river daily to Yangshuo carrying scores of tourists; most were Chinese though a few were Europeans. Many waved to me and by the second day when the boat crews recognised me they tooted their hooters and cheered, and slowed to avoid swamping me. After they had all passed, peace was restored and the waves diminished until only ripples lapped the sandy shores, and deep pools became mirrors for the pinnacles which towered into the sky.

Yangshuo was entertaining because my paddle-connector jammed again, and to try and unscrew it I resorted to greasing the joint with pork fat which I got from a café. It didn't work and most of the café's clientele tried their hands at it, with as many as six men at a time pulling and twisting from both ends of the paddle. Brute force also failed, and it wasn't until I tried using sewing machine oil, from a shoemaker, that the connector finally slid free.

The Lijiang River flows into the Pearl River and out to the South China Sea. With only three days left on my visa, I caught a bus downriver from Yangshuo to Wuzhou. The road, a minor one, led through a string of villages whose inhabitants were threshing rice in wooden threshing boxes, one for every few paddy-fields. One of the satisfying things about my journey through China is to have come out of the desert early in spring when plants are young, and watched them in the changing scenery becoming mature and ripening to gold. Harvesting was now going on throughout China; it was the culmination of a growing-season. I also felt seasoned and more complete. My journey had been fulfilling; and it seemed to have lasted longer than four months.

There were two more boat-rides yet to come, but now the canoe was a passenger too. After a full day jolting along on secondary roads we reached Wuzhou, where I hoped to catch an overnight steamer down the Pearl River to Canton. I was lucky to get the last sleeping-space left. These are arranged along a platform with low partitions to stop your neighbours rolling into your space. Each space has a porthole, open for the cooling breeze, and after I'd boarded the steamer I lay looking out at the wide river, hazy in the late sun. Wuzhou was a shambles of buildings propping each other up but with more charm than the new town across the river, despite its white pagoda.

My neighbour in the next berth was a heavyweight Han who managed to break the wooden partition by leaning on it. I shared my picnic supper with the family on my other side, and they gave me shrimps and home-cooked titbits. Everyone spoke Cantonese, which sounded harsh and raucous to my ears, and they could not understand my Mandarin. I slept well, and awoke to watch a pearly dawn and a small ferry with six swimming water-buffalo on ropes being led by its passengers.

By the time I disembarked in Canton it was raining. It was difficult to find the quay that serves the Hong Kong ferries, but fortunately when I got there they had space on the ferry that night. After a day in Canton I boarded it, and as we steamed away from the mainland, I said goodbye to China.

The three Polo travellers left China by sea. They must have had mixed feelings after seventeen years in the East. At first, the Khan had refused them permission to go home, saying that he liked them too much. But they knew that if they did not leave before the old Khan died, they could lose their travel facilities and protection. Also at that time, a princess was being sent by the Kublai Khan to the Khan of Persia, but because of Tartar wars along the overland route she would have to travel by sea. Fourteen ships were made ready, and the Khan was persuaded to let the Polos travel aboard them because, being Venetian, they had navigational skills.

They left in 1292, the voyage to Persia took two years and they arrived back in Venice in 1295. The story goes that their family didn't recognise them, which would hardly be surprising if they were dressed in travel-worn Tartar clothes and had almost forgotten how to speak the Venetian tongue. But human nature being what it is, when they showed the jewels they were carrying, their family began to recognise their lost relatives after all.

Just before the outbreak of the Second World War my grandmother left China on the Trans-Siberian railway. My mother had already left, travelling by ship with her nanny and school trunks, bound for England. I wondered what she would make of China today. To me it had been many things but above all an overwhelming emotional experience. I had travelled not as a passenger but as someone privileged to see beneath the multi-layered surfaces. The journey had left me exhausted but replete. Now I was ready for a new beginning.